Table of Cont

C000227766

Keto Sweet Eats Bonus

BONUS KETO SWEET EATS

I am delighted you have chosen my book to help you start or continue on your keto journey. Temptation by sweet treats can knock you off course so, to help you stay on the keto track, I am pleased to offer you three mini ebooks from my 'Keto Sweet Eats Series', completely free of charge! These three mini ebooks cover how to make everything from keto chocolate cake to keto ice cream to keto fat bombs so you don't have to feel like you are missing out, whatever the occasion. Simply visit the link below to get your free copy of all three mini ebooks:

http://ketojane.com/ketoworld

Ketogenic
GLOBAL KITCHEN

THE WORLD'S MOST DELICIOUS
FOODS MADE KETO & EASY

ELIZABETH JANE

Introduction

When non-ketogenic dieters buy a cookbook, they have a plethora of choices: Mediterranean, Asian, South American and Indian to name but a few. They literally have the world in their hands. When conducting a quick search on Amazon returns a list of "ketogenic cookbooks," these books tend to only offer "low-carb recipes" rather than any specific cuisine style. I wanted to bring the same choice of cookbooks to the ketogenic diet. You can now choose from French, Mexican and Indian low-carb recipes, among many others.

This recipe book showcases 100 delicious low-carb, keto-friendly recipes from all around the world. This book is designed with the idea of sharing as many variations of the ketogenic diet as possible to give you many options to choose from so low-carb eating never has to get boring. By combining flavors from around the world, your ketogenic meal plan will be full of exotic flavors and diversity, helping you stay the course and reach your health goals.

Just because the book is filled with worldly dishes, it does not mean that the ingredients can only be obtained by traveling the world. I have kept to ingredients that would be in most stores.

Recipe Notes

This book has been designed to include various regions, so you get flavors from around the world. Feel free to bounce around from region to region and not follow this book in any chronological order. Start with the recipes that intrigue you the most. There are a few additional perks to this book. Each recipe will contain a difficulty level as well as a price scale determining the level of expense for each recipe. The levels of difficulty and expense are relative within the book. All recipes are aimed to be accessible to the average person, there are no recipes which require a sous-chef or a small loan to make. Consider using the guides for occasions.

- Short on time? Go for the easy and cheaper meal options (more likely to have the ingredients at home).
- Entertaining? Try something a bit more complex and lavish to impress friends.

Each recipe is also labeled as to whether it's gluten-free or vegetarian. Although the majority of the recipes are gluten-free, due to the variations in certain product ingredients, not all recipes will be marked gluten-free. If you wish to make all recipes gluten-free be sure to check the food label on the ingredients you buy. I hope these new features in this book helps to make cooking these recipes that much easier.

Difficulty Level Key:

1: Easy - These recipes are perfect for when you need a quick yet satisfying meal.

2: Intermediate - These recipes work great when you have a little more time to commit to spending in the kitchen. These recipes are slightly more difficult to put together than the easy-level recipes but completely manageable for even beginner cooks.

3: More Difficult - For the adventurous aspiring chef looking to create something unique and take on a little bit of a challenge. These recipes are also ideal for when you are hosting a dinner party and are looking to impress your guests.

Cost Scale:

$: **Least Expensive -** Great recipes for everyday cooking.

$$: **Moderate -** Recipes that are middle of the road price-wise, but not too expensive.

$$$: **Most Expensive -** Ideal for making recipes for celebrations. Use these dishes for that special lunch or dinner.

Dietary Labels:

GF: Gluten-free

V: Vegetarian

Keto-Meter

This is something new that I have decided to include as I think it will be a great way to help you determine where each recipe stands on my custom made keto-meter. This will give you a better idea as far as how keto the recipe is VS how low carb the recipe is. I use calories from fat (%) to determine how keto each recipe is. You will see a label on each recipe indicating if a recipe falls within the low, medium, or high category.

Keto-meter key:

 L = Low keto - <30% of recipe calories are from fat

 M = Moderate keto – 30% - 60% of recipe calories are from fat

 H = High keto - >60% of recipe calories are from fat

Measurements

For avoidance of doubt, the measurements in each recipe should be interpreted as follows:

Tbsp. = tablespoon

tsp. = teaspoon

Cup = a US Cup

And lastly, if you enjoy this book, I would appreciate it if you would leave a review on Amazon. The below link will take you straight to the review page.

http://ketojane.com/GlobalKitchenReview

YOU MAY ALSO LIKE

Please visit the below link, for another books by the author

http://ketojane.com/books

The seasons change and so do your fat burning keto treats. Energize yourself all year round with sweet and savory goodness.

A Year of Fat Bombs: 52 Seasonal Sweet & Savory Recipes

★★★★½ ▾   70 customer reviews

52 delicious seasonal recipes keep you in ketosis when you fill the need to snack. Perfect to make ahead and snack on to the go.

Visit the link below to get your copy.

http://ketojane.com/bombs

On a keto or low carb diet and miss bread? Then this book is for you.

Keto Bread Bakers Cookbook

★★★★☆ ▾ 76

Learn to make low-carb homemade sandwich bread, bagels, muffins and more. All with natural ingredients and a great homemade taste. No experience or machine needed.

Visit the link below to get your copy.

http://ketojane.com/bread

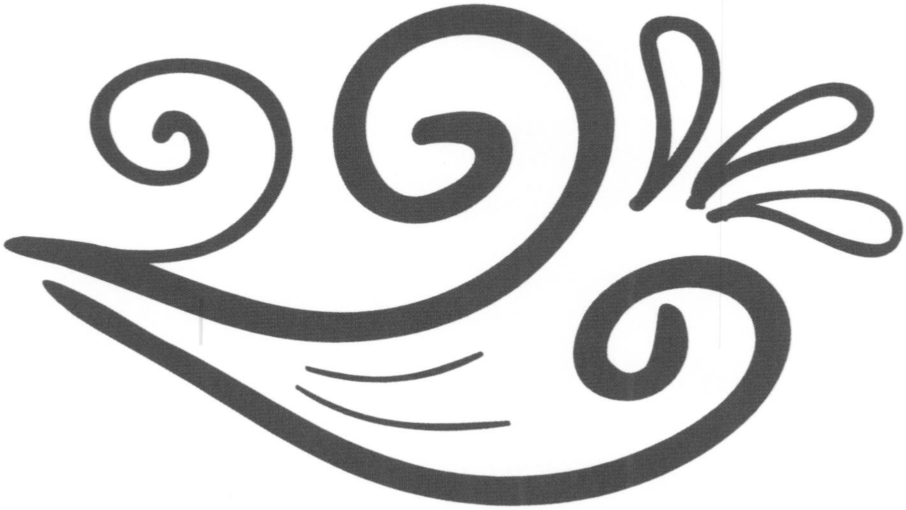

Table of Contents

Guide to the Symbols:

GF = Gluten Free

V = Vegetarian

L = Low keto - <30% of recipe calories are from fat

M = Moderate keto – 30% - 60% of recipe calories are from fat

H = High keto - >60% of recipe calories are from fat

Americas

Food from the Americas consists of a variety of flavors specific to each region. In this section of the book, you will find recipes from North America, South America, Central America, and the Caribbean.

South American food contains flavors traditionally inspired by Native American food traditions, African, and Spanish, as well as Italian. Depending on the specific country, the culinary flavors seen in South America vary greatly with many different varieties and flavors of which you will never get bored.

Here, you have delicious traditional South American dishes from Chile, Brazil, Argentina, Bolivia, and Peru covering a wide variety of different flavors. Chilean recipes tend to be on the spicy side, so if you are looking for ways to reduce the heat, try adding some unsweetened full-fat, Greek-style yogurt or avocado to balance out the spice. The remaining recipes you will see in this region provide you with a well-balanced combination of vegetable-based dishes, traditional meat plates and, of course, an authentic dessert.

The dishes featured in this region are vast and full of flavor. Explore each of the recipes to learn all about the array of different flavors used within this region's cuisine.

Southern-Style
MEATBALLS IN GRAVY (H)

HIGH KETO

SERVING SUGGESTION:
Serve with a side of steamed vegetables, such as broccoli or spinach and top with fresh parsley if desired.

Difficulty Level: 2 / **Cost:** $$
Preparation Time: 15 minutes
Cooking Time: 25 minutes
Serves: 5

NUTRITION FACTS
(Per Serving)

Calories from:
- Fat: 71%
- Protein: 24%
- Carb: 4%

Calories: 285
Total Carbs: 5g
Dietary Fiber: 2g
Protein: 17g
Total Fat: 22g
Net Carbs: 3g

Ingredients:

1 pound ground beef
1 egg
¼ cup almond flour
1 tsp. garlic powder
1 tsp. onion powder
1 Tbsp. fresh thyme
1 tsp. sea salt
1 Tbsp. tomato paste
1 Tbsp. olive oil
2 Tbsp. clarified butter
1 cup chopped onions
1 cup beef broth
¼ tsp. ground black pepper

Instructions:

1. Roll the ground beef into 15 golf ball-sized meatballs. Set aside.

2. Mix the almond flour, garlic powder, onion powder, thyme, sea salt, egg, and tomato paste in a mixing bowl. Add 1 meatball at a time to the mixture, making sure the meatball is covered.

3. Heat 1 tablespoon of olive oil in a large saucepan, and place the meatballs in the pan to fry. Cook for 3 minutes on each side until brown.

4. Add the beef broth, onions, ghee, and black pepper. Cover the pan, and simmer for 20 minutes.

Southern-Style
SPICY BACON
BURGER (H)

HIGH KETO

Difficulty Level: 2 / **Cost:** $$
Preparation Time: 20 minutes
Cooking Time: 15 minutes
Serves: 4

Ingredients:

1 pound ground beef
8 strips bacon
1 onion, peeled and sliced thinly
2 tomatoes, cored and chopped
2 jalapeño peppers, seeded and chopped
1 tsp. cumin
16 lettuce leaves
1 cup shredded cheddar cheese
2 Tbsp. coconut oil for cooking
1 low-carb bun (optional; not reflected in nutritional information)

Instructions:

1. Start by placing the ground beef into a mixing bowl with the chopped jalapeño peppers and cumin. Mix until combined. Form 8 small slider-sized patties out of the meat. Cook in a large skillet with the coconut oil for about 5 minutes each side or until cooked to your liking.

2. While the burgers are cooking, cook the bacon strips in a separate pan with coconut oil. Cook for about 10 minutes on each side or until crispy.

3. To form the burgers, using lettuce as the base, add the burger, cheddar cheese on top of the burger, and sliced onion. Then, add the sliced tomato and another lettuce leaf. Repeat with a second patty for a total of two per slider, topping with the 2 bacon strips per serving.

HIGH KETO

CAULIFLOWER
GRILLED CHEESE (GF, V, H)

NUTRITION FACTS

(Per Serving)

Calories from:

● Fat: 65%

● Protein: 20%

● Carb: 14%

Calories: 376
Total Carbs: 19g
Dietary Fiber: 6g
Protein: 19g
Total Fat: 27g
Net Carbs: 13g

READER RECOMMENDATION (ANNIE): Serve this with fresh salsa, it gives it a beautiful kick.

Difficulty Level: 2 / **Cost:** $$
Preparation Time: 20 minutes
Cooking Time: 25 minutes
Serves: 1

Ingredients:

½ head cauliflower, chopped roughly
1 egg, whisked
1 tsp. cayenne pepper
½ small onion, peeled and thinly sliced
½ green bell pepper, seeded and sliced
¼ cup shredded cheddar cheese
1 Tbsp. clarified butter

Instructions:

1. To make the cauliflower bread, place the cauliflower florets into a food processor with the cayenne pepper and process until it forms cauliflower "rice."

2. Transfer the cauliflower rice to a boiling pot with ¼ cup of water. Cover and steam for 5 minutes.

3. Transfer the cauliflower rice to a clean towel, and wring out the water. Transfer to a mixing bowl, and add the egg.

4. Place the cauliflower onto a lined baking sheet, and form into 2 "bread slices."

5. Bake at 450 degrees Fahrenheit for 15 minutes.

6. Add the cheese, onion, and bell pepper onto 1 slice and top with the second cauliflower bread slice carefully. Spread with the butter.

7. Cook for 10 minutes.

Kansas Cream
CHEESE-STYLE "HOT CAKES" (GF, V)

HIGH KETO

NUTRITION FACTS
(Per Serving)

Calories from:

● Fat: 91%

● Protein: 7%

● Carb: 2%

Calories: 213
Total Carbs: 1g
Dietary Fiber: 0g
Protein: 4g
Total Fat: 22g
Net Carbs: 1g

Difficulty Level: 1 / **Cost:** $
Preparation Time: 10 minutes
Cooking Time: 4 minutes
Serves: 4

Ingredients:

2 ounces cream cheese

2 eggs

½ tsp. gluten-free baking powder

½ tsp. vanilla extract

4 Tbsp. butter

4 Tbsp. sugar-free maple syrup
(optional; not reflected in nutritional
information)

1 Tbsp. coconut oil

Instructions:

1. Blend the cream cheese, eggs, baking powder, and vanilla extract together in a blender.

2. Pour into a heated skillet with coconut oil, and cook for about 1 minute each side.

3. Top with 1 tablespoon of butter each and 1 tablespoon of sugar-free maple syrup, if desired.

Pennsylvania STYLE MEAT-LOAF (GF, H)

HIGH KETO

Difficulty Level: 1 / **Cost:** $$
Prep. Time: 20 minutes
Cooking Time: 60 minutes
Serves: 6

NUTRITION
(Per Serving)

Calories from:
- Fat: 62%
- Protein: 33%
- Carb: 5%

Calories: 304
Total Carbs: 5g
Dietary Fiber: 1g
Protein: 24g
Total Fat: 20g
Net Carbs: 4g

Ingredients:

2 pounds ground beef
2 eggs
1 large onion, chopped
4 cloves garlic, chopped
1 handful fresh parsley
5 Tbsp. tomato paste
1 Tbsp. oregano
1 tsp. sea salt
2 Tbsp. butter and fresh rosemary for garnish

Instructions:

1. Start by preheating your oven to 425F.
2. Add the ground beef, eggs, garlic, onions, and parsley into a bowl and mix. Add 4 tablespoons of the tomato paste and stir.
3. Pour the meatloaf mixture into an oiled baking dish.
4. While the meatloaf is cooking, take the remaining 1 tablespoon of tomato paste, and water it down with 1 tablespoon of water to thin it out, set aside.
5. Cook for 1 hour, or until the meatloaf is cooked through. Coat with the watered-down tomato paste, and rosemary, if desired. Spread with fresh butter.

HIGH KETO

VIRGINIAN
CORNBREAD (GF, V, H)

Difficulty Level: 1 / **Cost:** $$
Prep. Time: 10 minutes
Cooking Time: 20 minutes
Serves: 6

NUTRITION
(Per Serving)

Calories from:

● Fat: 84%
● Protein: 13%
● Carb: 3%

Calories: 247
Total Carbs: 5g
Dietary Fiber: 3g
Protein: 8g
Total Fat: 23g
Net Carbs: 2g

Ingredients:

1 cup almond flour

1 tsp. baking powder

2 eggs

2 Tbsp. clarified butter

¼ cup full-fat cream cheese

Pinch of sea salt

Instructions:

1. Preheat the oven to 350F, and oil an 8x8 baking pan with 2 tablespoons of butter.

2. Combine all of the ingredients together by blending in a food processor or mixing by hand.

3. Pour the mixture into the baking dish, and bake for 15 to 20 minutes or until the top of the cornbread is golden brown.

MODERATE KETO

CARIBBEAN CHICKEN (GF, M)

Difficulty Level: 2 / **Cost:** $$
Preparation Time: 10 minutes
Cooking Time: 20 minutes
Serves: 4

NUTRITION FACTS
(Per Serving)

Calories from:

● Fat: 56%

● Protein: 40%

● Carb: 4%

Calories: 268
Total Carbs: 3g
Dietary Fiber: 0g
Protein: 27g
Total Fat: 17g
Net Carbs: 3g

Ingredients:

4 chicken breasts (with bone and skin)
1 red onion, peeled and chopped
4 Tbsp. melted coconut oil
1 Tbsp. soy sauce
1 Tbsp. lime zest
2 tsp. ground ginger
1 Tbsp. jalapeño pepper, seeded and chopped
Juice of 1 lime
1 lime, cut into wedges, for serving (optional)

Instructions:

1. Puree all of the ingredients in a food processor except for the chicken breasts.

2. Transfer the marinade to a bowl, and add the chicken breasts. Let this marinate for at least 2 hours in the refrigerator before cooking.

3. After the chicken has marinated, heat up your grill, and grill each side of the chicken for about 10 minutes or until the chicken is thoroughly cooked.

4. Serve with a fresh lime wedge, if desired.

HIGH KETO

JAMAICAN PATTIE (GF, H)

Difficulty Level: 2 / **Cost:** $$
Preparation Time: 20 minutes
Cooking Time: 30 minutes
Serves: 2

NUTRITION FACTS

(Per Serving)

Calories from:

● Fat: 67%
● Protein: 18%
● Carb: 14%

Calories: 307
Total Carbs: 13g
Dietary Fiber: 2g
Protein: 14g
Total Fat: 23g
Net Carbs: 11g

Ingredients:

2 eggs
½ cup coconut milk
2 Tbsp. coconut oil
½ cup coconut flour
½ tsp. baking powder
1 tsp. turmeric
½ pound ground beef
½ onion, peeled and chopped
1 pinch cumin
1 pinch salt and ground black pepper
1 jalapeño pepper, seeded and chopped

Instructions:

1. Whisk the milk and eggs until well combined.
2. Add the coconut oil and coconut flour and whisk. Add the turmeric, salt, and black pepper. Mix until smooth.
3. Sauté the onion in a pan with the ground beef, cumin, and chopped jalapeño pepper. Cook until the meat is no longer pink.
4. Preheat your oven to 350 degrees, and line a baking sheet with parchment paper.
5. Take the dough and make 4 balls, and roll the dough flat onto the baking sheet. Add the beef mixture on two pieces of the dough.
6. Place one piece of the dough over another to create 2 large Jamaican patties, and press down to seal the edges.
7. Bake for 30 minutes.

COCONUT SLUSH DESSERT (GF, V, H)

HIGH KETO

Difficulty Level: 1 / **Cost:** $ **Prep. Time:** 5 min
Cooking Time: None **Serves:** 1

Ingredients:

1 cup coconut cream
½ cup sugar-free pineapple sparkling water
Juice of 1 lemon
Handful of ice
Shredded coconut, for topping (optional)

Instructions:

1. Place all of the ingredients except for the shredded coconut into a high-speed blender and blend until smooth.
2. Top with shredded coconut, if desired.

PEPPER POT SOUP (GF, H)

HIGH KETO

Difficulty Level: 1 / **Cost:** $ **Prep. Time:** 10 minutes
Cooking Time: 30 minutes **Serves:** 6

Ingredients:

2 Tbsp. olive oil
4 scallions, chopped
2 garlic cloves, peeled and minced
1 onion, peeled and chopped
1 cup fresh spinach
4 cups chicken broth
1 jalapeño pepper, seeded

Instructions:

1. Place all of the ingredients in a large stockpot and bring to a boil.
2. Reduce to a simmer and cook for 30 minutes.
3. Blend until smooth using an immersion blender.

NUTRITION FACTS
(Per Serving)

Calories from:
- Fat: 62%
- Protein: 37%
- Carb: 1%

Calories: 568
Total Carbs: 4g
Dietary Fiber: 3g
Protein: 51g
Total Fat: 38g
Net Carbs: 1g

BLACKENED SALMON (GF, H)

 HIGH KETO

Difficulty Level: 2 / **Cost:** $$$ **Prep. Time:** 20 mins
Cooking Time: 25 minutes **Serves:** 2

Ingredients:

2 salmon fillets
1 avocado
1 Tbsp. mayonnaise
1 Tbsp. blackening spice
1 cup lettuce
1 pinch sea salt

Instructions:

1. Mash the avocado and add the mayonnaise, mixing until combined.
2. Preheat the grill.
3. While the grill is heating up, rub the seasonings on both sides of the salmon fillets, and place them on the grill. Grill for about 5 minutes per side or until cooked.
4. Serve over lettuce and top with the avocado sauce.

DEVILED EGGS (GF, V, H)

HIGH KETO

NUTRITION FACTS
(Per Serving)

Calories from:
- Fat: 74%
- Protein: 22%
- Carb: 4%

Calories: 109
Total Carbs: 1g
Dietary Fiber: 0g
Protein: 6g
Total Fat: 9g
Net Carbs: 1g

Difficulty Level: 1 / **Cost:** $ **Prep. Time:** 10 minutes
Cooking Time: 15 minutes **Serves:** 3

Ingredients:

3 large hard-boiled eggs
1 Tbsp. full-fat mayonnaise
1 tsp. Dijon mustard
½ tsp. paprika
Salt and ground black pepper, to taste
Dill, for garnish

Instructions:

1. Slice the hard-boiled eggs in half and remove the yolk.
2. Place the yolk in a mixing bowl and mash together with the remaining ingredients except for the salt and black pepper. Taste and add a pinch of salt or black pepper, if needed.
3. Fill the egg white with the yolk mixture.
4. Chill for at least 1 hour before serving and garnish with fresh dill.

Chocolate COVERED CANDIED BACON (GF, H)

HIGH KETO

Difficulty Level: 2 / **Cost:** $$
Prep. Time: 15 minutes
Cooking Time: 20-25 mins
Serves: 4 (7 squares each)

NUTRITION FACTS
(Per Serving)

Calories from:
- Fat: 73%
- Protein: 15%
- Carb: 12%

Calories: 284
Total Carbs: 9g
Dietary Fiber: 2g
Protein: 12g
Total Fat: 25g
Net Carbs: 7g

Ingredients:

6 slices of uncured bacon
½ cup sugar-free maple syrup
½ tsp. pure vanilla extract
¼ cup sugar-free dark
chocolate chips
2 Tbsp. coconut oil
½ tsp. sea salt + more
for serving

Instructions:

1. Start by preheating the oven to 350 degrees Fahrenheit and lining a baking sheet with parchment paper.
2. Combine the maple syrup, vanilla and ½ tsp. salt in a small bowl and whisk to combine.
3. Dip the bacon strips into the mixture coating both sides and place on the parchment lined baking sheet.
4. Bake for 20-25 minutes or until the bacon is crispy.
5. Five minutes before the bacon is done cooking, place the chocolate chips and coconut oil into a small stockpot over low heat and whisk until melted. Remove from heat.
6. Once the bacon is cooked, allow it to cool and then cut into 1-inch squares, making 28 total.
7. Dip the bacon squares into the chocolate and place back on the parchment lined baking sheet, or if needed into a smaller parchment lined container.
8. Refrigerate for 30 minutes to set.
9. Serve chilled and store leftovers in the fridge.

Chilean-Style
GUACAMOLE
(GF, V, H)

HIGH KETO

Difficulty Level: 1 / **Cost:** $$
Preparation Time: 10 minutes
Cooking Time: None
Serves: 4

NUTRITION FACTS
(Per Serving)

Calories from:

- Fat: 85%
- Protein: 7%
- Carb: 9%

Calories: 259
Total Carbs: 16g
Dietary Fiber: 11g
Protein: 4g
Total Fat: 22g
Net Carbs: 5g

Ingredients:

2 avocados, pitted and scooped
1 Roma tomato, diced
½ onion, peeled and chopped
1 jalapeño pepper, seeded and diced
2 Tbsp. lemon juice
Handful fresh cilantro, chopped
1 tsp. red pepper flakes

Instructions:

1. Place all ingredients in a mixing bowl and mash everything together with the avocado. Refrigerate for 30 minutes to chill before serving.

SPICY
EMPANADA (GF, H)

HIGH KETO

Difficulty Level: 2 / **Cost:** $$
Preparation Time: 30 minutes
Cooking Time: 10 minutes
Serves: 8

NUTRITION FACTS
(Per Serving)

Calories from:
- Fat: 81%
- Protein: 15%
- Carb: 4%

Calories: 291
Total Carbs: 5g
Dietary Fiber: 2g
Protein: 11g
Total Fat: 26g
Net Carbs: 3g

Ingredients:

1 cup almond meal
2 Tbsp. butter, melted
½ tsp. salt
½ tsp. baking powder
⅓ cup full-fat coconut milk
¼ cup water
2 cup shredded cheese of choice
4 small jalapeño peppers, seeded and chopped
2 Tbsp. coconut oil
Fresh salsa, if desired

Instructions:

1. Whisk the almond meal, salt, and baking powder into a large mixing bowl. Add the melted butter, whisk until combined, and set aside.

2. Bring the water and coconut milk to a boil, and pour into the flour mix, stirring until all the clumps are gone. Knead the dough, divide into 8 portions, and roll into a ball.

3. Place ¼ cup of shredded cheese and ½ of a jalapeño pepper into the center of the dough ball, and then fold one side over, covering the shredded cheese. Press down to seal the edges.

4. Preheat a large skillet over medium heat with the coconut oil, and cook the empanadas for about 1 or 2 minutes until lightly browned on each side.

5. Serve with fresh salsa, if desired.

Chilean-Style
CORN ON
THE COB (GF, V, H)

HIGH KETO

Difficulty Level: 1 / **Cost:** $$
Preparation Time: 10 minutes
Cooking Time: None
Serves: 4

NUTRITION FACTS
(Per Serving)

Calories from:
- Fat: 74%
- Protein: 8%
- Carb: 18%

Calories: 401
Total Carbs: 18g
Dietary Fiber: 2g
Protein: 8g
Total Fat: 33g
Net Carbs: 16g

Ingredients:

2 small ears of corn
2 Tbsp. butter
½ tsp. cumin
1 tsp. paprika
½ cup cream cheese, for serving
Thinly sliced green onion, for serving

Instructions:

1. Remove the husks from the corn, and bring a large pot of water to a boil. Add the 2 ears of corn and cook for about 10 minutes or until the corn is tender.

2. While the corn is cooking, whisk together the cumin, paprika, and salt in a small bowl.

3. Cover the corn with a slab of butter, and season with the paprika mix. Garnish with thinly sliced green onion.

4. For a traditional Chilean side dish, serve the corn with ¼ cup cream cheese per serving.

NUTRITION FACTS
(Per Serving)

Calories from:
- Fat: 77%
- Protein: 4%
- Carb: 19%

Calories: 206
Total Carbs: 15g
Dietary Fiber: 6g
Protein: 3g
Total Fat: 16g
Net Carbs: 9g

Chilean PEPPER SALSA (GF, V, H)

HIGH KETO

Difficulty Level: 1 / **Cost:** $$ **Prep. Time:** 10 minutes
Cooking Time: None **Serves:** 5

Ingredients:

2 green jalapeño peppers, seeded
2 avocados, pitted and scooped
¼ cup canned corn, rinsed and drained
4 garlic cloves, peeled
½ tsp. black peppercorns
1 onion, peeled and chopped
4 tomatoes, cored and chopped
3 Tbsp. olive oil
Fresh cilantro, for garnish

Instructions:

1. Place all ingredients except for the cilantro into a food processor and pulse but not until completely smooth. You just want it blended enough to chop up the veggies.
2. Garnish with cilantro.
3. Serve with sliced vegetables, such as carrots, cucumbers, or celery, for a low-carb snack.

Brazilian CHEESE BREAD (GF, V, H)

Difficulty Level: 1 / **Cost:** $$ **Prep. Time:** 5 minutes
Cooking Time: 15 minutes **Serves:** 8

NUTRITION FACTS
(Per Serving)

Calories from:
- Fat: 85%
- Protein: 11%
- Carb: 4%

HIGH KETO

Calories: 321
Total Carbs: 6g
Dietary Fiber: 3g
Protein: 9g
Total Fat: 31g
Net Carbs: 3g

Ingredients:

1 egg
¼ cup melted coconut oil
½ cup heavy cream
1½ cup almond flour
½ cup feta cheese
1 tsp. salt

Instructions:

1. Preheat your oven to 400F and coat a muffin tin with oil.
2. Blend all of the ingredients together in a blender and pour the mixture into 8 muffin cups.
3. Bake for 15 minutes or until golden brown.

COLLARD GREENS (GF, V, H)

HIGH KETO

NUTRITION FACTS
(Per Serving)

Calories from:
- Fat: 87%
- Protein: 6%
- Carb: 6%

Calories: 64
Total Carbs: 2g
Dietary Fiber: 1g
Protein: 1g
Total Fat: 6g
Net Carbs: 1g

SERVING SUGGESTION:
Serve with chicken breast, or another lean protein source

Difficulty Level: 1 / **Cost:** $ **Prep. Time:** 5 minutes
Cooking Time: 10 minutes **Serves:** 4

Ingredients:

4 cups collard greens
2 Tbsp. butter
1 clove garlic, peeled minced
2 tsp. cayenne pepper
1 tsp. salt

Instructions:

1. Rinse and pat collard greens dry using paper towel. Remove the stems and cut the leaves into small strips.

2. Add the butter to a large skillet, and add the collards, garlic, and seasonings. Sauté until the collard greens begin to wilt, which will take between 5 and 10 minutes.

Brazilian "RICE" (GF, V, H)

Difficulty Level: 1 / **Cost:** $ **Prep. Time:** 15 minutes
Cooking Time: 10 minutes **Serves:** 4

NUTRITION FACTS
(Per Serving)

Calories from:
- Fat: 53%
- Protein: 13%
- Carb: 34%

MODERATE KETO

Calories: 131
Total Carbs: 15g
Dietary Fiber: 5g
Protein: 4g
Total Fat: 7g
Net Carbs: 10g

Ingredients:

1 large head of cauliflower, cut into florets
1 cup chopped onion
3 garlic cloves, peeled and minced
2 Tbsp. coconut oil
1 cup carrots, peeled and chopped
2 tsp. paprika
1 tsp. coriander
1 tsp. salt
1 tsp. ground black pepper
Fresh cilantro, for garnish

Instructions:

1. Place the cauliflower florets into a large pot over medium heat with a ¼ cup of water. Steam for 7 to 9 minutes or until tender. Place the steamed cauliflower into a large clean towel and wring out all of the excess water. Transfer to a food processor.

2. Add all of the remaining ingredients, and pulse until the cauliflower turns to "rice".

3. Serve with fresh cilantro.

HIGH KETO

CILANTRO CHIMICHURRI (GF, V, H)

Difficulty Level: 1 / **Cost:** $
Prep. Time: 5 minutes
Cooking Time: None
Serves: 5

NUTRITION
(Per Serving)

Calories from:
- Fat: 100%
- Protein: 0%
- Carb: 0%

Calories: 98
Total Carbs: 0g
Dietary Fiber: 0g
Protein: 0g
Total Fat: 11g
Net Carbs: 0g

Ingredients:

½ cup cilantro

¼ cup olive oil

2 tsp. lime juice

2 cloves garlic, peeled

1 Tbsp. onion powder

¼ tsp. red pepper flakes

1 handful of fresh parsley.

Instructions:

1. Place all of the ingredients in a blender and blend until smooth.

2. Serve with veggies or as a marinade.

Argentinian

MILANESA (GF, V, H)

HIGH KETO

Difficulty Level: 2 / **Cost:** $$
Preparation Time: 60 minutes
Cooking Time: 10 minutes
Serves: 8

NUTRITION FACTS
(Per Serving)

Calories from:

● Fat: 73%

● Protein: 16%

● Carb: 11%

Calories: 292
Total Carbs: 16g
Dietary Fiber: 8g
Protein: 11g
Total Fat: 23g
Net Carbs: 8g

Ingredients:

2 eggplants

2 eggs

1 cup arugula

3 Tbsp. unsweetened almond milk

3 cloves garlic, peeled and chopped

2 cups almond meal

2 Tbsp. nutritional yeast

Sea salt, to taste

SERVING SUGGESTION:
Serve with a side of salad greens, sliced tomato, and avocado.

Instructions:

1. Peel and slice the eggplant into 8 thick strips, sprinkle with salt and let sit for 20 minutes.

2. While the eggplant is sitting out, whisk together the eggs, milk, and garlic. After the eggplant has sat out for 30 minutes, add the eggplant strips to the egg mixture and let it marinate in the fridge for 30 minutes.

3. Preheat your oven to 400F, and line a baking sheet with parchment paper.

4. While the oven is preheating, add the almond meal and nutritional yeast to a mixing bowl, and dunk the marinated eggplant into the almond meal to cover until well coated. Transfer to the baking sheet.

5. Bake for 5 minutes on each side, until the eggplant is lightly browned. Serve with fresh arugula.

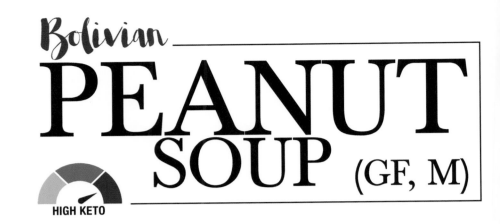

Bolivian
PEANUT SOUP (GF, M)

HIGH KETO

Difficulty Level: 1 / **Cost:** $
Preparation Time: 10 minutes
Cooking Time: 3 hours
Serves: 6

NUTRITION FACTS
(Per Serving)

Calories from:
- Fat: 88%
- Protein: 8%
- Carb: 4%

Calories: 339
Total Carbs: 4g
Dietary Fiber: 1g
Protein: 7g
Total Fat: 33g
Net Carbs: 3g

Ingredients:

1 large onion, peeled and diced
2 carrots, peeled and sliced into thick rounds
½ cup green peas
½ cup tomatoes, diced
4 cups beef stock
½ cup raw peanuts, ground in a blender
1 head of cauliflower, cut into florets
Salt and ground black pepper, to taste
Hot pepper sauce, for serving
Chopped green onions, for serving

Instructions:

1. Place all of the ingredients in a slow cooker except for the hot sauce and green onion. Cook on high for 3 hours.

2. Puree the soup until smooth using an immersion blender.

PIQUE MACHO

MODERATE KETO

(Spicy Bolivian Beef) (GF, M)

Difficulty Level: 2 / **Cost:** $$
Preparation Time: 10 minutes
Cooking Time: 15 minutes
Serves: 4

NUTRITION FACTS
(Per Serving)

Calories from:

○ Fat: 51%
● Protein: 42%
● Carb: 7%

Calories: 353
Total Carbs: 8g
Dietary Fiber: 2g
Protein: 36g
Total Fat: 19g
Net Carbs: 6g

Ingredients:

1 pound of beef steak, cut into thick chunks or strips
½ white onion, peeled and diced
4 stalks green onion, sliced in half
1 tomato, cored and chopped
1 small red bell pepper, seeded and cut into chunks
1 small green bell pepper, seeded and cut into chunks
1 small yellow bell pepper, seeded and cut into chunks
2 chili peppers, thinly sliced
2 garlic cloves, peeled and chopped
½ tsp. ground cumin
1 Tbsp. coconut oil, for cooking
Salt and ground black pepper, to taste

Instructions:

1. Start by heating a large skillet over medium heat with the coconut oil. Add the steak and cook on both sides until cooked to your liking.

2. Add the bell peppers, chili peppers, garlic, tomato, onion, green onions, and seasoning. Sauté for another 5 minutes.

3. Scoop onto 4 separate serving plates and sprinkle with paprika for a traditional Bolivian flavor.

Bolivian

COCONUT
FLAM (GF, V, H)

HIGH KETO

Difficulty Level: 1 / **Cost:** $
Preparation Time: 20 minutes
Cooking Time: 40 minutes
Serves: 8

NUTRITION FACTS
(Per Serving)

Calories from:
- Fat: 88%
- Protein: 8%
- Carb: 4%

Calories: 339
Total Carbs: 4g
Dietary Fiber: 1g
Protein: 7g
Total Fat: 33g
Net Carbs: 3g

Ingredients:

1 cup coconut cream

2 cups heavy cream

1 tsp. cornstarch

8 eggs

2 drops liquid stevia

Strawberries, sliced, for serving

Instructions:

1. Bring the coconut cream and heavy cream to a boil, add the stevia, and stir. Add the cornstarch and stir again. Remove from the stove and cool.

2. Whisk the egg yolks into the mixture, and whip the egg whites in a separate bowl until soft peaks form.

3. Fold the egg whites into the mixture.

4. Cook on very low heat for about 40 minutes. After it is done cooking, remove from heat, pour into a small baking dish, and chill in the refrigerator until it solidifies. The dessert should be a jelly-like consistency when done.

5. Scoop like you would ice cream, and serve with 2 sliced strawberries per serving.

READER RECOMMENDATION (JOAN):
I associate this dessert with sweetness and recommend adding in some extra stevia.

Peruvian
SHRIMP CEVICHE SALAD (GF, M)

MODERATE KETO

NUTRITION FACTS
(Per Serving)

Calories from:

○ Fat: 31%

◑ Protein: 51%

● Carb: 18%

Calories: 89

Total Carbs: 5g

Dietary Fiber: 1g

Protein: 11g

Total Fat: 3g

Net Carbs: 4g

SERVING SUGGESTION: Serve with a side of spicy salsa for an added kick.

Difficulty Level: 1 / **Cost:** $$
Preparation Time: 15 minutes
Cooking Time: 10 minutes
Serves: 6

Ingredients:

1 pound shrimp, peeled and deveined

1 red onion, peeled and sliced

4 Tbsp. lime juice

1 Tbsp. thinly sliced chili peppers

1 red bell pepper, seeded and chopped

1 tsp. garlic, chopped

1 tsp. Peruvian pepper paste (aji Amarillo)

Handful of fresh cilantro

1 Tbsp. coconut oil, for cooking

Instructions:

1. Heat a large skillet over medium heat with the coconut oil. Add all of the ingredients except for the lime juice and cilantro, and cook until the shrimp have turned pink.

2. Serve on a large platter and drizzle with lime juice. Garnish with cilantro.

HIGH KETO

SUSPIRO LIMENO
(Peruvian Dessert Custard) (V, H)

Difficulty Level: 2 / **Cost:** $$
Preparation Time: 10 minutes
Cooking Time: 15 minutes
Serves: 4

NUTRITION FACTS
(Per Serving)

Calories from:
- Fat: 92%
- Protein: 4%
- Carb: 4%

Calories: 279
Total Carbs: 4g
Dietary Fiber: 1g
Protein: 3g
Total Fat: 29g
Net Carbs: 3g

READER RECOMMENDATION (JOAN):
I associate this dessert with sweetness and recommend adding in some extra stevia.

Ingredients:

4 cups unsweetened coconut milk

1 cup of full-fat coconut cream

2 eggs (yolks only)

2 drops stevia extract

1 tsp. pure vanilla extract

Sugar-free chocolate sauce, for serving (optional; not reflected in nutritional information)

Instructions:

1. Whisk the coconut milk, and vanilla in a bowl. Whisk in the egg yolks, and add to a saucepan. Cook over medium heat for 30 minutes or until the mixture thickens. Pour into a baking dish.

2. Whip the coconut cream with the stevia until soft peaks form. Spread this mixture over the milk mixture, and chill in the refrigerator until cold.

3. Serve in individual serving dishes and drizzle with sugar-free chocolate sauce, if desired.

NUTRITION FACTS
(Per Serving)

Calories from:
- Fat: 28%
- Protein: 66%
- Carb: 6%

Calories: 131
Total Carbs: 2g
Dietary Fiber: 0g
Protein: 21g
Total Fat: 4g
Net Carbs: 2g

Puerto Rican CRAB MEAT (L)

LOW KETO

Difficulty Level: 2 / **Cost:** $$ **Prep. Time:** 10 minutes
Cooking Time: 7 minutes **Serves:** 4

Ingredients:

1 pound lump crab meat
½ white onion, peeled and thinly chopped
2 cloves garlic, peeled and minced
½ tsp. dried oregano
1 tsp. hot pepper sauce
1 Tbsp. freshly chopped cilantro (optional, for garnish)
1 Tbsp. coconut oil for cooking

SERVING SUGGESTION: Mix ½ cup of dry white wine with 2 tablespoons of coconut aminos to use in the base of a serving bowl. Add the crab meat mixture on top of the sauce.

Instructions:

1. Heat a large skillet over medium heat with the coconut oil, and add all of the ingredients except for the cilantro. Sauté for 5 to 7 minutes.

2. Transfer the crab mixture into a bowl and top with cilantro, if desired.

Puerto Rican SHRIMP SALAD (GF, H)

HIGH KETO

NUTRITION FACTS
(Per Serving)

Calories from:
- Fat: 63%
- Protein: 32%
- Carb: 6%

Calories: 221
Total Carbs: 5g
Dietary Fiber: 2g
Protein: 17g
Total Fat: 15g
Net Carbs: 3g

Difficulty Level: 1 / **Cost:** $ **Prep. Time:** 10 minutes
Cooking Time: None **Serves:** 2

Ingredients:

4 cups dark leafy greens, chopped
½ pound jumbo shrimp, peeled, deveined, cooked, and chilled.
8 grape tomatoes, sliced
Paprika, for garnish
2 Tbsp. olive oil

READER RECOMMENDATION (STELLA): If you love mayo, swap the salad cream out. This gives the salad a great creamy texture.

Instructions:

1. Place the salad greens on the base of 2 serving plates and top with the sliced tomatoes, shrimp and a dash of paprika

2. Drizzle with olive oil.

Puerto Rican LOW-CARB RUM BALLS (V, H)

HIGH KETO

Difficulty Level: 2 / **Cost:** $$
Preparation Time: 10 minutes
Cooking Time: 15 minutes
Serves: 4

NUTRITION FACTS
(Per Serving)

Calories from:

- Fat: 70%
- Protein: 9%
- Carb: 20%

Calories: 275
Total Carbs: 16g
Dietary Fiber: 3g
Protein: 6g
Total Fat: 20g
Net Carbs: 13g

Ingredients:

1 cup cashews
1 cup chopped walnuts
⅓ cup cocoa powder
½ cup rum
4 Tbsp. sugar-free maple syrup
½ cup shredded coconut, for topping

Instructions:

1. Place the nuts and cocoa powder into a food processor and blend until combined.
2. Add the sugar-free maple syrup and rum and blend until the mixture comes together.
3. Form into 8 "rum balls" and roll into the shredded coconut.
4. Store in the refrigerator and chill before serving.

MODERATE KETO

Cuban COCONUT
FAJITA CHICKEN (GF, M)

Difficulty Level: 2 / **Cost:** $$
Preparation Time: 10 mins
Cooking Time: 1 hour 10 mins
Serves: 4

NUTRITION FACTS
(Per Serving)

Calories from:

● Fat: 51%

● Protein: 44%

● Carb: 5%

Calories: 251
Total Carbs: 5g
Dietary Fiber: 2g
Protein: 27g
Total Fat: 14g
Net Carbs: 3g

SERVING SUGGESTION: Serve the coconut chicken over a bed of lettuce for a delicious Cuban-style salad.

Ingredients:

4 boneless and skinless chicken breasts

½ white onion, peeled and thinly chopped

1 red bell pepper, seeded and chopped

1 yellow bell pepper, seeded and chopped

1 green bell pepper, seeded and chopped

½ can full-fat coconut milk

1 Tbsp. coconut oil

1 pinch red pepper flakes

Instructions:

1. Preheat your oven to 425F, and coat a baking dish with coconut oil.

2. In a large skillet, sauté the chicken with the onion and bell peppers until the chicken and vegetables begin to brown. Add the coconut milk and stir.

3. Transfer the chicken mixture into the baking dish and bake for about 45 minutes or until the chicken is cooked through and tender and the coconut milk has completely cooked down.

4. Season with red pepper flakes.

RECETA DE BISTEC ENCEBOLLADO
(Cuban Steak With Onions) (M)

MODERATE KETO

NUTRITION FACTS
(Per Serving)

Calories from:
- Fat: 44%
- Protein: 39%
- Carb: 16%

Calories: 259
Total Carbs: 12g
Dietary Fiber: 2g
Protein: 24g
Total Fat: 12g
Net Carbs: 10g

Difficulty Level: 1 / **Cost:** $$
Preparation Time: 10 minutes
Cooking Time: 10 minutes
Serves: 4

SERVING SUGGESTION: Serve with a side of tomatoes and arugula for added nutritional value.

READER RECOMMENDATION (JOANNE): This is a fantastic recipe, but adding a little heavy cream put it in the 'wonderful' category.

Ingredients:

1 pound sirloin steak, cut into 4 servings
2 cloves garlic, peeled and chopped
1 tsp. adobo seasoning
¼ cup vinegar
3 large red onions, peeled and thinly sliced

Instructions:

1. In a large mixing bowl, mix the garlic, adobo seasoning, and vinegar together.
2. Add the steak to the seasoning mix and marinate for 30 minutes.
3. While the steak is marinating, sauté the onions in a large skillet over medium heat with coconut oil until translucent. Set aside once cooked.
4. Cook the steaks in the same sauté pan that you used for the onions and cook until they reach the desired doneness. Serve with the onions.

Cuban
MERINGUE
PUFFS (GF, V, L)

LOW KETO

Difficulty Level: 1 / **Cost:** $
Prep. Time: 10 minutes
Cooking Time: 30 minutes
Serves: 8

NUTRITION FACTS
(Per Serving)

Calories from:

- Fat: 26%
- Protein: 63%
- Carb: 11%

Calories: 70
Total Carbs: 2g
Dietary Fiber: 0g
Protein: 11g
Total Fat: 2g
Net Carbs: 2g

Ingredients:

3 cups egg whites at room temperature (for easy measuring use egg white from an egg white carton so you can easily measure out 3 cups without having to separate the yolks from the whites!)

3 tsp. stevia

½ cup shredded coconut

1 ½ Tbsp. vinegar

1 tsp. coconut extract

Instructions:

1. Preheat your oven to 275 and line a baking sheet with parchment paper.

2. Beating the egg whites until fluffy.

3. Mix in the stevia, coconut, vinegar, and coconut extract and continue to beat until well combined.

4. Drop onto the baking sheet with parchment paper and bake for 30 minutes. This should make approximately 8 puffs.

Asia

Asian cuisine includes traditionally inspired recipes from China, Japan, Korea, Indonesia, the Philippines, and South Asia, which includes the Indian subcontinent. Traditional flavors of Central and Eastern Asia include sesame, garlic, ginger and chili, with meat and fish being a popular addition to many recipes. Southeast Asia features Indian-inspired recipes often consumed in Indonesia with curried-based dishes as well as Thai-inspired flavors.

This book has taken Asian-inspired recipes and kept the traditional flavors while creating low-carb, ketogenic-friendly dishes. You can expect to see plenty of chilies, garlic, and curry spices used in these recipes as well as low-carb swaps for traditionally breaded or flour-added foods. The Indian-inspired dishes tend to be on the spicy side, so I would recommend adding some yogurt to help cool off the spice.

I hope you find the flavors of Asian to give your ketogenic diet a creative and delicious boost.

Indian
FLARE-ROASTED LAMB (GF, H)

HIGH KETO

Difficulty Level: 2 / **Cost:** $$$
Prep. Time: 10 minutes
Cooking Time: 20 minutes
Serves: 2

NUTRITION
(Per Serving)

Calories from:
- Fat: 75%
- Protein: 25%
- Carb: 0%

Calories: 592
Total Carbs: 0g
Dietary Fiber: 0g
Protein: 36g
Total Fat: 49g
Net Carbs: 0g

Ingredients:

4 lamb chops
1 tsp. masala powder
¼ tsp. ground black pepper
¼ tsp. garlic powder
¼ tsp. onion powder
2 Tbsp. extra virgin olive oil
2 Tbsp. sour cream
Fresh thyme, for topping (optional)

Instructions:

1. Marinate the lamb chops for a few hours or up to 24 hours before you decide to cook them. Place the lamb chops, sour cream, olive oil, and all of the seasonings into a large baking dish. Rub the mixture to cover the lamb chops, and place in the refrigerator to marinate.

2. When ready to cook, add the lamb chops with additional oil to a skillet, and cook on low heat for about 25 minutes or until the lamb is well browned on the outside.

3. Transfer to a serving plate, and top with fresh thyme, if desired.

Indian
CURRIED
SHRIMP (GF, M)

MODERATE KETO

Difficulty Level: 1 / **Cost:** $$
Preparation Time: 10 mins
Cooking Time: 10 mins
Serves: 4

NUTRITION FACTS
(Per Serving)

Calories from:

● Fat: 32%   Calories: 145
● Protein: 45%   Total Carbs: 10g
● Carb: 23%   Dietary Fiber: 2g
Protein: 16g
Total Fat: 5g
Net Carbs: 8g

Ingredients:

1 pound deveined shrimp
2 seedless oranges, quartered
1 Tbsp. melted coconut oil
1 Tbsp. curry powder
¼ tsp. ground cinnamon
¼ tsp. ground black pepper
1 pinch sea salt
Chopped cilantro for garnish

Instructions:

1. Heat a skillet over medium heat with the coconut oil and add the shrimp. Cook for about 5 minutes, and then add the quartered orange slices, curry powder, cinnamon, salt, and black pepper. Continue to cook until the shrimp are pink and begin to curl and the oranges are browned.

2. Serve the shrimp and oranges on a kabob.

Indian-Style
ICE CREAM
"KULFI" (GF, V, H)

HIGH KETO

READER RECOMMENDATION (JOAN): I associate this dessert with sweetness and recommend adding in some extra stevia.

Difficulty Level: 1 / **Cost:** $$
Prep. Time: 10 minutes
Cooking Time: 0 minutes
Serves: 8

NUTRITION
(Per Serving)

Calories from:
- Fat: 90%
- Protein: 6%
- Carb: 4%

Calories: 392
Total Carbs: 5g
Dietary Fiber: 1g
Protein: 6g
Total Fat: 40g
Net Carbs: 4g

Ingredients:

1¼ cups full-fat coconut milk
1¼ cups heavy cream
2 cups whipped cream cheese
½ tsp. green tea powder
¼ tsp. xanthan gum
Fresh mint leaf, for topping

Instructions:

1. Place all of the ingredients in a high-speed blender and blend until smooth.

2. Transfer to a freezer-safe container. Freeze overnight.

3. Remove from the freezer and scoop just as you would regular ice cream. Top with a fresh mint leaf, if desired.

INDIA

KADHAI MURGHI
(Indian-Style CHICKEN AND VEGGIE STIR-FRY (GF, M)

MODERATE KETO

NUTRITION FACTS
(Per Serving)

Calories from:
- Fat: 52%
- Protein: 40%
- Carb: 8%

Calories: 324
Total Carbs: 11g
Dietary Fiber: 5g
Protein: 31g
Total Fat: 18g
Net Carbs: 6g

Difficulty Level: 2 / **Cost:** $$
Preparation Time: 20 minutes
Cooking Time: 20 minutes
Serves: 4

Ingredients:

1 tsp. cumin

½ tsp. curry powder

¼ tsp. turmeric

½ tsp. red pepper flakes

4 Tbsp. olive oil

4 boneless, skinless chicken breasts,
cut into strips

1 eggplant, sliced into rounds

1 yellow bell pepper, seeded and
chopped

1 red bell pepper, seeded and
chopped

2 garlic cloves, peeled and crushed

Peeled and sliced onion

Lettuce, for garnish

Fresh rosemary, for garnish

Instructions:

1. Start by making the marinade for the chicken by mixing the olive oil, cumin, curry powder, turmeric, and red pepper flakes. Add the chicken strips to the marinade, and let them sit for 30 minutes.

2. While the chicken is marinating, chop the bell peppers, eggplant, and garlic. Set aside.

3. After 30 minutes, heat a large skillet over medium heat, and add the marinated chicken. Cook for about 5 minutes each side, and then add the vegetables. Continue to cook until the peppers and eggplant are tender and the chicken is cooked through.

4. Serve with lettuce, sliced onion, and rosemary if desired.

Indian CURRIED DRINK (GF, V, H)

HIGH KETO

(Per Serving)

Calories from:
- Fat: 92%
- Protein: 3%
- Carb: 5%

Calories: 339
Total Carbs: 7g
Dietary Fiber: 3g
Protein: 3g
Total Fat: 36g
Net Carbs: 4g

Difficulty Level: 1 / **Cost:** $$ **Prep. Time:** 10 minutes
Cooking Time: 5 minutes **Serves:** 2

Ingredients:

1 cup coconut milk
1 tsp. turmeric powder
¼ tsp. ground black pepper
¼ tsp. ground cinnamon
1 Tbsp. coconut oil

Instructions:

1. Place all of the ingredients in a stockpot over low heat and whisk until combined. Heat on low until warm.
2. Serve in a coffee mug.

EASY CURRIED CAULIFLOWER STEAKS (GF, V, L)

NUTRITION FACTS

(Per Serving)

Calories from:
- Fat: 15%
- Protein: 33%
- Carb: 52%

Calories: 69
Total Carbs: 13g
Dietary Fiber: 5g
Protein: 5g
Total Fat: 1g
Net Carbs: 8g

LOW KETO

Difficulty Level: 1 / **Cost:** $ **Prep. Time:** 10 minutes
Cooking Time: 5 minutes **Serves:** 3

Ingredients:

1 large head of cauliflower
2 Tbsp. curry powder
¼ tsp. red pepper flakes
2 Tbsp. unsweetened Greek yogurt
Freshly chopped basil, for garnish

Instructions:

1. Remove the leaves from the cauliflower, cut off the base core, and cut into thick "steak"-like strips.
2. Place all of the cauliflower strips into a microwave-safe bowl and add the Greek yogurt and seasoning. Mix until well combined.
3. Microwave for about 5 minutes or until tender.
4. Serve with freshly chopped basil, if desired.

Thai CHICKEN SOUP (GF, H)

HIGH KETO

Difficulty Level: 1 / **Cost:** $$
Preparation Time: 10 mins
Cooking Time: 30 mins
Serves: 4

NUTRITION FACTS
(Per Serving)

Calories from:
- Fat: 72%
- Protein: 17%
- Carb: 11%

Calories: 430
Total Carbs: 17g
Dietary Fiber: 5g
Protein: 19g
Total Fat: 35g
Net Carbs: 12g

Ingredients:

2 chicken breasts, thinly sliced

1 (15-ounce) can coconut milk

1 onion, peeled and chopped

3 garlic cloves, peeled and minced

6 cups chicken broth

2 Tbsp. green curry paste

1 Tbsp. fish sauce

2 carrots, peeled and cut into crescents

1 zucchini, cut into rounds

Pinch of sea salt

1 Tbsp. olive oil

Instructions:

1. Heat a large stockpot over medium heat and add the olive oil. Start to sauté the onion for 2 to 4 minutes. Add the garlic and sauté for another minute.

2. Add the remaining ingredients and bring to a boil.

3. Simmer for 20 to 25 minutes or until the chicken is cooked through and the vegetables are tender.

4. Serve right away.

Vietnamese
FRIED SESAME
CAKE (GF, V, H)

HIGH KETO

READER RECOMMENDATION (JOAN):
I associate this dessert with sweetness and recommend adding in some extra stevia.

READER RECOMMENDATION (DAVE)
If you have a sweet tooth (like me), top with sugar free maple syrup.

Difficulty Level: 1 / **Cost:** $$
Preparation Time: 10 mins
Cooking Time: 5 mins
Serves: 8

NUTRITION FACTS
(Per Serving)

Calories from:
- Fat: 84%
- Protein: 12%
- Carb: 4%

Calories: 199
Total Carbs: 6g
Dietary Fiber: 4g
Protein: 6g
Total Fat: 18g
Net Carbs: 2g

Ingredients:

1 egg

¼ cup water

1 ½ Tbsp. melted butter

1 cup almond flour

1 tsp. baking soda

½ cup white sesame seeds, for coating

Peanut oil, for frying (note that this is not calculated into the nutrition information)

Instructions:

1. Mix the egg, water and melted butter. Whisk until well combined.

2. Add the almond flour and baking soda and knead until it all comes together.

3. Form the dough into 8 balls and roll into the sesame seeds until covered.

4. Fill a large stockpot at least ¼ of the way with the peanut oil and heat over low heat.

5. Place the dough balls into the oil. Fry until the dough becomes a light brown color.

6. Transfer onto a paper towel to drain.

(Per Serving)

Calories from:

● Fat: 89%
● Protein: 4%
● Carb: 7%

HIGH KETO

Calories: 105
Total Carbs: 3g
Dietary Fiber: 1g
Protein: 1g
Total Fat: 11g
Net Carbs: 2g

Vietnamese
ICED COFFEE
DESSERT (GF, V, H)

Difficulty Level: 1 / **Cost:** $ **Prep. Time:** 5 minutes
Cooking Time: None **Serves:** 1

Ingredients:

2 Tbsp. coarsely ground Vietnamese coffee, brewed with ½ cup of boiling water
2 Tbsp. full-fat unsweetened coconut cream, plus more for serving
1 pinch ground cinnamon
1 drop liquid stevia
Handful of ice

Instructions:

1. Pour the 2 tablespoons of coconut cream into the bottom of a large mug.
2. Pour the brewed Vietnamese coffee into the mug, along with the stevia.
3. Add the pinch of cinnamon and a handful of ice cubes.
4. Top with a dollop of coconut cream.

Indonesian
SPICY
CHICKEN (GF, M)

MODERATE KETO

(Per Serving)

Calories from:

● Fat: 55%
● Protein: 37%
● Carb: 9%

Calories: 244
Total Carbs: 7g
Dietary Fiber: 2g
Protein: 21g
Total Fat: 14g
Net Carbs: 5g

Difficulty Level: 2 / **Cost:** $$ **Prep. Time:** 15 minutes
Cooking Time: 20 minutes **Serves:** 4

Ingredients:

8 chicken wings
1 tsp. turmeric
¼ cup dried red chili peppers
4 garlic cloves, peeled and chopped
1-inch ginger root, grated
5 whole cloves, ground
1 tsp. ground cinnamon
2 tomatoes, cored and chopped
4 Tbsp. tomato paste
½ cup water
Rosemary (optional)

Instructions:

1. Start by making the spice paste by pureeing the chili peppers, garlic, onion, tomatoes, and ginger together in a food processor.
2. Cook the chicken in a large skillet with the coconut oil until well browned on both sides. Add the cloves and cinnamon, and then the tomato paste and water, and simmer for about 15 minutes or until the chicken is cooked through and the water has cooked down. Add the spice paste and stir.
3. Serve with a pinch of fresh rosemary, if desired.

Coconut INDONESIAN MUFFINS (GF, V, H)

HIGH KETO

Difficulty Level: 1 / **Cost:** $$
Preparation Time: 15 mins
Cooking Time: 30 mins
Serves: 12

NUTRITION FACTS
(Per Serving)

Calories from:

- Fat: 86%
- Protein: 8%
- Carb: 6%

Calories: 261
Total Carbs: 8g
Dietary Fiber: 4g
Protein: 5g
Total Fat: 25g
Net Carbs: 4g

Ingredients:

2½ cups coconut milk

1¼ cup almond meal

2 cups shredded coconut

1 tsp. salt

Vegetable oil, for coating muffin tin

Instructions:

1. Preheat your oven to 375F, and grease a 12-cup muffin tin.

2. Add all of the ingredients to a mixing bowl and stir until smooth.

3. Spoon the muffin batter into the muffin tins, and bake for about 30 minutes or until the top is golden brown.

Philippine-Style
SLOW COOKER
ADOBO CHICKEN (GF, M)

MODERATE KETO

NUTRITION FACTS
(Per Serving)

Calories from:
- Fat: 53%
- Protein: 40%
- Carb: 6%

Calories: 402
Total Carbs: 7g
Dietary Fiber: 1g
Protein: 39g
Total Fat: 23g
Net Carbs: 6g

Difficulty Level: 2 / **Cost:** $$
Preparation Time: 10 minutes
Cooking Time: 4 hours
Serves: 5

Ingredients:

8 skinless chicken thighs, cubed

2 onions, peeled and sliced

2 cloves garlic, peeled and chopped

¼ cup low-sodium soy sauce

2 cups chicken broth

2 tsp. paprika

1 cup chopped bok choy

½ cup apple cider vinegar

Instructions:

1. Combine the broth, chicken, onion, garlic, soy sauce, paprika, and apple cider vinegar in a slow cooker. Cook on high for 4 hours.

2. Add the bok choy and cook for an additional 10 minutes.

SERVING SUGGESTION:
For an added boost of flavor, serve with a side of steamed vegetables.

Filipino RIBS (GF, H)

HIGH KETO

Difficulty Level: 2 / **Cost:** $$
Preparation Time: 15 mins
Cooking Time: 1 hour + 45 mins
Serves: 5

SERVING SUGGESTION: Serve with a side of steamed vegetables or an arugula salad.

NUTRITION FACTS
(Per Serving)

Calories from:
- Fat: 67%
- Protein: 30%
- Carb: 3%

Calories: 290
Total Carbs: 2g
Dietary Fiber: 0g
Protein: 21g
Total Fat: 21g
Net Carbs: 2g

Ingredients:

2 pounds pork spare ribs
2 Tbsp. low-sodium soy sauce
1 star anise
1 tsp. ground ginger
2 Tbsp. Worcestershire sauce
1 Tbsp. lemon juice

Instructions:

1. Place the ribs into a large stockpot with the star anise. Cover with water, and bring to a boil. Cover and let simmer for about 1 hour and 15 minutes, or until the ribs are tender.

2. Mix the soy sauce, ginger, lemon juice, and Worcestershire sauce.

3. After the ribs have finished cooking, add them to a large baking sheet, and preheat the oven to 400F. Cover the ribs with the marinade mixture, and cook for about 30 minutes or until the marinade begins to glaze.

NUTRITION FACTS
(Per Serving)

Calories from:
- Fat: 53%
- Protein: 10%
- Carb: 37%

Calories: 131
Total Carbs: 16g
Dietary Fiber: 5g
Protein: 3g
Total Fat: 7g
Net Carbs: 11g

Quick & Easy
ASIAN SALAD (GF, V, M)

MODERATE KETO

Difficulty Level: 1 / **Cost:** $$ **Prep. Time:** 10 minutes
Cooking Time: 5 minutes **Serves:** 2

Ingredients:

2 cups shredded carrots
2 cups shredded green cabbage
2 green onions, chopped
Juice of 1 lime
1-inch piece of fresh ginger, finely grated
½ cup shiitake mushrooms, sliced
1 Tbsp. olive oil, for cooking

Instructions:

1. Sauté all of the ingredients together in the olive oil over medium heat except for the lime juice. Sauté for 3 to 5 minutes or until the cabbage begins to wilt.
2. Transfer to 2 serving dishes and drizzle with the fresh lime juice.

Korean
SHORT RIBS (H)

HIGH KETO

NUTRITION FACTS
(Per Serving)

Calories from:
- Fat: 79%
- Protein: 19%
- Carb: 1%

Calories: 351
Total Carbs: 1g
Dietary Fiber: 0g
Protein: 17g
Total Fat: 31g
Net Carbs: 1g

Difficulty Level: 2 / **Cost:** $$ **Prep. Time:** 12 hours
Cooking Time: 2 hours **Serves:** 4

Ingredients:

1 pound short ribs
¼ cup coconut aminos
1 Tbsp. rice vinegar
1 tsp. sesame oil
1 Tbsp. garlic powder
¼ cup water

Instructions:

1. Place all of the ingredients except for the ribs and water into a mixing bowl and whisk. Refrigerate for at least 12 hours.
2. After 12 hours of chilling, add the short ribs to the sauce mixture and let marinate for 30 minutes. Remove the ribs from the sauce and store the sauce in the refrigerator.
3. Preheat your oven to 250F, and place the ribs into a large oven-safe baking dish with the water. Cook for 1½ hours.
4. Baste the ribs with the marinade and cook for another 30 minutes or until the meat begins to pull away from the bones on the ribs.

MODERATE KETO

GENERAL
TSO'S CHICKEN (M)

Difficulty Level: 2 / **Cost:** $$
Preparation Time: 15 minutes
Cooking Time: 10 minutes
Serves: 5

NUTRITION FACTS
(Per Serving)

Calories from:
- Fat: 57%
- Protein: 42%
- Carb: 1%

Calories: 355
Total Carbs: 3g
Dietary Fiber: 2g
Protein: 36g
Total Fat: 22g
Net Carbs: 1g

Ingredients:

6 boneless and skinless chicken breasts, cubed
½ cup almond flour
1 egg
3 Tbsp. coconut oil
2 Tbsp. chicken broth
2 Tbsp. rice vinegar
2 Tbsp. soy sauce
¼ tsp. sesame oil
½ tsp. onion powder
1 tsp. red pepper flakes
1 pinch ground ginger
Green onions, for garnish

Instructions:

1. In a large bowl, combine the rice vinegar, soy sauce, sesame oil, chicken broth, red pepper flakes, onion powder, and ginger and set aside.

2. In a separate bowl, whisk the egg and set aside.

3. In another bowl, add the almond flour.

4. Take the chicken cubes, dip them into the almond flour and cover on both sides. Dip into the egg mixture to cover. Add to the dressing mixture to thoroughly cover both sides.

5. In a large sauté pan, heat the oil over medium heat, then add the leftover soy sauce mixture and a pinch of almond flour to thicken up the sauce a bit.

6. Add the chicken cubes and sauté for about 7 minutes on each side or until well browned and cooked through.

7. Serve with green onions, if desired.

Asian
GINGER
LETTUCE WRAPS (H)

MODERATE KETO

Difficulty Level: 2 / **Cost:** $$
Preparation Time: 10 mins
Cooking Time: 15 minutes
Serves: 4

NUTRITION FACTS
(Per Serving)

Calories from:

- Fat: 60%
- Protein: 33%
- Carb: 7%

Calories: 229
Total Carbs: 4g
Dietary Fiber: 0g
Protein: 20g
Total Fat: 16g
Net Carbs: 4g

Ingredients:

1 pound ground chicken

4 Tbsp. soy sauce

1 Tbsp. hoisin sauce

1 Tbsp. rice wine vinegar

1 Tbsp. ground ginger

2 garlic cloves, peeled and chopped

1 Tbsp. sriracha sauce (optional)

8 large butterhead lettuce leaves

2 Tbsp. coconut oil

Instructions:

1. Start by preheating a large skillet over medium heat with coconut oil, and add the ground chicken. Begin to brown for 5 minutes.

2. Add all of the remaining ingredients except the lettuce, and continue to sauté for 5 to 7 minutes or until the chicken is well cooked.

3. Serve in lettuce cups.

EAST ASIA

MODERATE KETO

BEEF AND
BROCCOLI (M)

Difficulty Level: 2 / **Cost:** $$
Preparation Time: 15 minutes
Cooking Time: 10 minutes
Serves: 4

NUTRITION FACTS
(Per Serving)

Calories from:
- Fat: 45%
- Protein: 40%
- Carb: 15%

Calories: 296
Total Carbs: 12g
Dietary Fiber: 1g
Protein: 30g
Total Fat: 15g
Net Carbs: 11g

Ingredients:

½ cup low-sodium soy sauce
¼ cup cornstarch
½ Tbsp. freshly grated ginger
1 Tbsp. garlic powder
1 pound flank steak, sliced thinly
2 Tbsp. peanut oil
2 cups broccoli florets
2 Tbsp. fish sauce
¼ cup shredded cabbage, for garnish

Instructions:

1. Put the sliced beef in a mixing bowl and set aside.

2. In a separate bowl, add the soy sauce, fish sauce, cornstarch, ginger, and garlic. Pour ½ of this mixture over the beef.

3. Heat a large skillet over medium heat with 1 tablespoon of peanut oil and add the broccoli. Sauté for 2 minutes and then place on a serving plate.

4. In the same skillet, pour the rest of the remaining 1 tablespoon of peanut oil and add the beef. Cook for about 1 minute on each side until brown.

5. Add the remaining sauce mixture, and cook on high heat until the sauce starts to thicken.

6. Add the broccoli back to the skillet and stir to combine.

7. Serve on 4 different serving plates, and top with shredded cabbage, if desired.

EAST ASIA

GARLIC
SHRIMP (M)

MODERATE KETO

Difficulty Level: 2 / **Cost:** $$
Preparation Time: 10 minutes
Cooking Time: 10 minutes
Serves: 3

NUTRITION FACTS
(Per Serving)

Calories from:
- Fat: 38%
- Protein: 47%
- Carb: 15%

Calories: 185
Total Carbs: 7g
Dietary Fiber: 0g
Protein: 22g
Total Fat: 8g
Net Carbs: 7g

Ingredients:

1 pound peeled and deveined shrimp, tails left on
2 Tbsp. fish sauce
1 Tbsp. soy sauce
1 tsp. sesame oil
1 Tbsp. cornstarch
4 garlic cloves, peeled and chopped
2 green onions, finely chopped, for garnish
1 Tbsp. peanut oil, for cooking

Instructions:

1. Whisk together the fish sauce, soy sauce, sesame oil, garlic, and cornstarch in a mixing bowl until smooth.

2. Preheat a large skillet over medium heat with the peanut oil. Once heated, add the shrimp and sauté for 3 to 5 minutes, flipping the shrimp halfway through.

3. Pour in the sauce mixture and simmer for 5 minutes or until the sauce starts to thicken up.

4. Serve topped with freshly chopped green onions.

Europe

European cuisine is so broad that surely you have tried flavors from a handful of these countries. In this book, a few of the countries covered include cuisines from England, Ireland, Italy, Greece, and Belgium, giving you a look at a wide variety of different ways to make ketogenic eating fun and diverse.

There will be traditional European dessert recipes featured with predominantly meat-based entrees. You will experience traditional carb-based Irish recipes turned keto style, traditional British fish and chips without the flour, and Italian flavors without the heavy carbs. Traditional Mediterranean-flavored dishes are also featured in this region with a Greek flair and even Scandinavian cuisine ranging from Norway, Sweden, Finland, and Iceland.

As a serving suggestion, many of the keto-style dessert recipes inspired by cuisine from the United Kingdom, would pair deliciously with a cup of tea.

Enjoy your flavorful tour around Europe and be amazed at how some of the most traditionally carb-loaded foods can be turned into a delicious ketogenic treat.

NUTRITION FACTS
(Per Serving)

Calories from:
- Fat: 48%
- Protein: 44%
- Carb: 8%

Calories: 206
Total Carbs: 4g
Dietary Fiber: 0g
Protein: 23g
Total Fat: 11g
Net Carbs: 4g

MODERATE KETO

Greek LAMB WITH MINT TZATZIKI (GF, M)

Difficulty Level: 2 / **Cost:** $$ **Prep. Time:** 15 minutes
Cooking Time: 15 minutes **Serves:** 4

Ingredients:

2 cups boneless leg of lamb, cooked and cubed
½ tomato, cored and diced
1 cup full-fat Greek yogurt
1 Tbsp. fresh mint leaves
½ cucumber, chopped
2 cloves garlic, peeled and minced
1 pinch sea salt
4 large lettuce leaves

Instructions:

1. Mix the yogurt, cucumber, mint, tomato, and garlic together in a mixing bowl. Stir until combined. Season with salt to taste.
2. Place the small pieces of lamb onto individual skewers, and use the tzatziki as the dip.

Greek LEMON ALMOND MUFFINS (GF, V, H)

NUTRITION FACTS
(Per Serving)

Calories from:
- Fat: 71%
- Protein: 17%
- Carb: 12%

Calories: 151
Total Carbs: 4g
Dietary Fiber: 2g
Protein: 7g
Total Fat: 13g
Net Carbs: 5g

HIGH KETO

Difficulty Level: 1 / **Cost:** $$ **Prep. Time:** 10 minutes
Cooking Time: 20 minutes **Serves:** 8

Ingredients:

4 eggs
2 tsp. stevia
1 cup almond meal
1 tsp. gluten-free baking powder
1 tsp. pure vanilla extract
1½ Tbsp. lemon juice
½ Tbsp. lemon zest

Instructions:

1. Preheat the oven to 350F, and grease a muffin tin with oil or butter.
2. Mix all of the ingredients together with a handheld mixer or in a blender and mix until smooth.
3. Transfer the muffin mix evenly into 8 muffin cups and bake for about 20 minutes or until lightly browned.

READER RECOMMENDATION (DAVE)
This works great as a breakfast - serve with grated almonds and a slab of butter for a savory delight.

French
RATATOUILLE
(GF, M)

MODERATE KETO

Difficulty Level: 1 / **Cost:** $
Preparation Time: 10 minutes
Cooking Time: 45 minutes
Serves: 4

NUTRITION FACTS
(Per Serving)

Calories from:
- Fat: 59%
- Protein: 11%
- Carb: 30%

Calories: 119
Total Carbs: 13g
Dietary Fiber: 5g
Protein: 3g
Total Fat: 7g
Net Carbs: 8g

Ingredients:

½ cup Vidalia onions, chopped

3 garlic cloves, peeled and chopped

2 Tbsp. olive oil

1 eggplant, chopped

1 zucchini, chopped

1 cup beef broth

Fresh thyme, for garnish

Instructions:

1. Preheat your oven to 375F, and pour the beef broth into the bottom of a baking dish.

2. Line the dish with the eggplant and garlic and drizzle 1 tablespoon olive oil.

3. Top that layer with the zucchini and onions. Drizzle the remaining 1 tablespoon olive oil.

4. Cover and bake for 45 minutes.

5. Garnish with fresh thyme.

READER RECOMMENDATION (LINDA):
Using vegetable broth makes this yummy and vegetarian friendly.

Escargot In
PARSLEY
HERB BUTTER (H)

HIGH KETO

Difficulty Level: 1 / **Cost:** $$
Preparation Time: 8 hours
Cooking Time: 10 mins
Serves: 4

NUTRITION FACTS
(Per Serving)

Calories from:

Fat: 92%
Protein: 6%
Carb: 2%

Calories: 469
Total Carbs: 2g
Dietary Fiber: 0g
Protein: 7g
Total Fat: 48g
Net Carbs: 2g

Ingredients:

1 cup butter

1 handful of chopped parsley

1 Tbsp. French brandy

3 cloves garlic, peeled and minced

24 large snail shells

24 canned snails

Instructions:

1. In a large bowl, mix the butter, parsley, garlic, and brandy and chill for 8 hours.

2. Preheat your oven to 400F, and line a large baking sheet with parchment paper.

3. Scoop the parsley herb mixture into each snail shell to fill halfway, and then add a snail. Add more parsley herb mix to fill the shell. Continue this step for the rest of the snail shells.

4. Bake for 10 minutes.

CHOCOLATE *Belgian* WAFFLE (V, H)

HIGH KETO

Difficulty Level: 1 / **Cost:** $$
Preparation Time: 30 minutes
Cooking Time: 10 minutes
Serves: 3

NUTRITION FACTS
(Per Serving)

Calories from:
- Fat: 74%
- Protein: 11%
- Carb: 15%

Calories: 319
Total Carbs: 14g
Dietary Fiber: 2g
Protein: 9g
Total Fat: 26g
Net Carbs: 12g

SERVING SUGGESTION:
The amount of waffles served per serving will depend on the size of your waffle maker or how big you make your waffles. Simply divide the total amount into three and enjoy!

Ingredients:

5 Tbsp. melted butter

3 eggs

¼ cup buttermilk

⅓ cup coconut flour

1 tsp. gluten-free baking powder

1 Tbsp. cocoa powder

Sugar-free maple syrup for topping (optional; not reflected in nutritional information)

Instructions:

1. Place all of the ingredients except for the maple syrup into a blender and blend until the mix is very smooth. Let this sit out for 20 minutes to thicken.

2. Heat your waffle maker, and cook the waffles according to the waffle maker instructions. Continue until the batter is used up.

3. If you do not have a waffle maker and you want to make Belgian pancakes, cook the batter as you would pancakes on a large nonstick pan.

READER RECOMMENDATION (JOAN):
I associate this dessert with sweetness and recommend adding in some extra stevia.

Belgian
CHOCOLATE
MOUSSE (GF, V, H)

HIGH KETO

Difficulty Level: 1 / **Cost:** $
Prep. Time: 10 minutes
Cooking Time: 5 minutes
Serves: 3

NUTRITION
(Per Serving)

Calories from:
- Fat: 82%
- Protein: 12%
- Carb: 6%

Calories: 259
Total Carbs: 8g
Dietary Fiber: 4g
Protein: 8g
Total Fat: 24g
Net Carbs: 4g

READER RECOMMENDATION (JOAN):
I associate this dessert with sweetness and recommend adding in some extra stevia.

Ingredients:

1 can full-fat coconut milk

3 Tbsp. raw cocoa powder

3 eggs

Mint leaf, for garnish (optional)

Instructions:

1. Refrigerate the coconut milk the night before you want to make this recipe. The next morning, remove only the hardened part of the milk and add this to a stockpot.

2. Add the eggs and cocoa powder and whisk over low heat until combined and the coconut cream has softened.

3. Chill before serving, and then serve in 3 individual dessert bowls.

4. Add a mint leaf as garnish, if desired.

MODERATE KETO

COMBO
LASAGNA (GF, M)

Difficulty Level: 2 / **Cost:** $$
Preparation Time: 25 mins
Cooking Time: 40 mins
Serves: 5

NUTRITION FACTS
(Per Serving)

Calories from:

○ Fat: 52%   Calories: 467
● Protein: 37%   Total Carbs: 17g
● Carb: 11%   Dietary Fiber: 4g
                         Protein: 42g
                         Total Fat: 26g
                         Net Carbs: 13g

Ingredients:

1 pound ground beef

1 pound ground turkey

1 jar low-sugar marinara sauce

1 cup shredded mozzarella cheese

½ tsp. paprika

1 tsp. Italian seasoning

4 zucchini

2 Tbsp. olive oil, plus extra to coat baking dish

Pinch salt and ground black pepper, to taste

Fresh basil and thyme, for garnish

Instructions:

1. Sauté the ground beef with 1 tablespoon of olive in a large pan, and sauté the turkey in a separate pan with another tablespoon of olive oil.

2. While the meats are cooking, slice the zucchini into thick strips using a mandoline, and place 6 strips across the bottom of an oiled baking dish. Top the first layer with ½ of the marinara sauce.

3. Continue to sauté the meats until cooked, stirring occasionally. Once cooked, combine the meats in one pan, and add the paprika, salt, black pepper, and Italian seasoning.

4. Scoop half of the mixture over the marinara sauce, and top with the remaining strips of zucchini. Top this layer with the remainder of the sauce, meat, and all of the cheese.

5. Bake at 350F for 15 to 20 minutes, or until the cheese starts to bubble.

6. Garnish with basil and thyme

Italian
CHICKEN
CASSEROLE (GF, M)

MODERATE KETO

Difficulty Level: 1 / **Cost:** $$
Preparation Time: 15 minutes
Cooking Time: 20 minutes
Serves: 4

NUTRITION FACTS
(Per Serving)

Calories from:
- Fat: 48%
- Protein: 49%
- Carb: 3%

Calories: 282
Total Carbs: 2g
Dietary Fiber: 0g
Protein: 34g
Total Fat: 15g
Net Carbs: 2g

Ingredients:

1 pound chicken tenders

1 Tbsp. ground black pepper

1 Tbsp. oregano

1 cup shredded mozzarella cheese

1 cup cherry tomatoes, cut in half

2 Tbsp. olive oil

Salt, to taste

Instructions:

1. Preheat your oven to 425F, and grease a baking dish with coconut oil. Start by marinating the chicken tenders with the olive oil, black pepper, and oregano.

2. Transfer the chicken tenders to the baking dish and top with the cherry tomatoes and shredded mozzarella cheese.

3. Bake for 20 to 25 minutes or until the chicken tenders are cooked through and the cheese has melted.

4. Season with salt to taste.

SERVING SUGGESTION: Serve with a side of fresh arugula.

ITALY

VANILLA
GELATO (GF, V, H)

HIGH KETO

Difficulty Level: 1 / **Cost:** $$
Preparation Time: 8 hours
Cooking Time: 10 mins
Serves: 4

NUTRITION FACTS

(Per Serving)

Calories from:

● Fat: 90%
● Protein: 5%
● Carb: 4%

Calories: 542
Total Carbs: 9g
Dietary Fiber: 3g
Protein: 7g
Total Fat: 55g
Net Carbs: 6g

Ingredients:

2 cups coconut milk

1 cup heavy cream

4 egg yolks

3 drops vanilla crème stevia extract

2 tsp. pure vanilla extract

Instructions:

1. In a saucepan over medium heat, heat the coconut milk and heavy cream until warm.

2. In a separate bowl, whisk the egg yolks with the stevia extract and vanilla, and pour in the warm milk mixture slowly.

3. Return the milk and egg mixture to the saucepan, and stir continuously over low heat until the mixture gels.

4. Strain through a fine strainer into a bowl and chill overnight.

5. The next day, pour the mixture into an ice cream maker, and make according to the manufacturer's instructions. Transfer into a freezer-safe container and freeze until the gelato hardens.

SERVING SUGGESTION:
Serve with fresh mint leaves for an added kick of flavor.

Irish SODA BREAD (GF, V, H)

HIGH KETO

Difficulty Level: 2 / **Cost:** $$
Prep. Time: 15 minutes
Cooking Time: 35 minutes
Serves: 8

NUTRITION
(Per Serving)

Calories from:
- Fat: 81%
- Protein: 13%
- Carb: 6%

Calories: 379
Total Carbs: 13g
Dietary Fiber: 7g
Protein: 12g
Total Fat: 34g
Net Carbs: 6g

READER RECOMMENDATION (JOAN): Try adding a pinch of cinnamon and cutting the wedges before baking to make the bread seem more like scones! Also try adding less stevia and a bit of salt for a more savory Irish Soda Bread flavor that is not as sweet.

Ingredients:

2 cups almond flour
½ cup ground flaxseeds
2 tsp. powdered stevia
2 tsp. gluten-free baking powder
3 Tbsp. butter
2 eggs
¼ cup heavy cream
¼ cup currants

Instructions:

1. Preheat the oven to 350F.
2. Add the flaxseeds, stevia, baking powder, and butter to a food processor and pulse.
3. Add the remaining ingredients except for the currants.
4. Transfer the dough into a mixing bowl and add the currants.
5. Shape the dough, and place it on an oven-safe, oiled baking sheet.
6. Bake for 35 minutes or until the top of the bread is golden brown.
7. Cool before slicing and serve with butter, if desired.

Irish LAMB STEW (GF, H)

HIGH KETO

Difficulty Level: 2 / **Cost:** $$
Preparation Time: 20 minutes
Cooking Time: 30 minutes
Serves: 6

NUTRITION FACTS
(Per Serving)

Calories from:
- Fat: 65%
- Protein: 26%
- Carb: 9%

Calories: 309
Total Carbs: 8g
Dietary Fiber: 1g
Protein: 20g
Total Fat: 22g
Net Carbs: 7g

Ingredients:

8 small lamb chops
1 onion, peeled and chopped
1 tsp. black peppercorns
1 tsp. fresh rosemary
1 tsp. fresh thyme
1 leek, chopped (white part only)
1 cup button mushrooms
4 garlic cloves, peeled and minced
4 cups vegetable broth
1 cup chopped carrots
1 Tbsp. coconut oil

Instructions:

1. Start by heating a large skillet over medium heat with the coconut oil and brown the lamb chops. Add the leek and garlic and cook for another 3 minutes.

2. Add all of the ingredients including the lamb, leek, and garlic to a large stockpot and simmer for 25 minutes.

READER RECOMMENDATION (DAISY):
I tried adding a few sauces to this, by far my favorite was a dollop of sour cream!

CLASSIC *Irish* GROUND SAUSAGE (GF, H)

HIGH KETO

Difficulty Level: 1 / **Cost:** $$
Prep. Time: 20 minutes
Cooking Time: 15 minutes
Serves: 4

NUTRITION
(Per Serving)

Calories from:
- Fat: 68%
- Protein: 32%
- Carb: 0%

Calories: 364
Total Carbs: 0g
Dietary Fiber: 0g
Protein: 29g
Total Fat: 27g
Net Carbs: 0g

Ingredients:

1 pound lean ground pork
1 tsp. all spice
1 tsp. salt
1 tsp. ground black pepper
½ tsp. dried marjoram
Coconut oil, for cooking

Instructions:

1. Sauté the pork with the spices in a large skillet with coconut oil until well-cooked or form into patties and cook as part of a traditional Irish breakfast dish.

CLASSIC *Irish* COFFEE (V, H)

Difficulty Level: 1 / **Cost:** $
Prep. Time: 5 minutes
Cooking Time: 5 minutes
Serves: 1

NUTRITION
(Per Serving)

Calories: 133
Total Carbs: 0g
Dietary Fiber: 0g
Protein: 0g
Total Fat: 3g
Net Carbs: 0g

Ingredients:

1 cup strong black coffee
1 ounce Irish whiskey
1 tsp. vanilla crème stevia extract
1 Tbsp. whipped cream
Whole coffee beans, for garnish
(optional)

Instructions:

1. Stir the Irish whiskey and stevia together in the base of a coffee mug. Add the hot coffee.

2. Top with fresh whipped cream.

3. Add a few coffee beans for garnish, if desired.

British FISH
AND CHIPS (GF, M)

MODERATE KETO

Difficulty Level: 2 / **Cost:** $$
Preparation Time: 20 minutes
Cooking Time: 10 minutes
Serves: 4

NUTRITION FACTS
(Per Serving)

Calories from:
- Fat: 55%
- Protein: 38%
- Carb: 7%

Calories: 303
Total Carbs: 7g
Dietary Fiber: 2g
Protein: 28g
Total Fat: 18g
Net Carbs: 5g

Ingredients:

Fish:
5 Tbsp. coconut flour
4 eggs
¼ cup heavy cream
1 tsp. onion powder
1 tsp. gluten-free baking powder
2 cups peanut oil, for frying (not reflected in nutritional information)
1 pound tilapia filets, cut into small chunks

Chips:
Leftover batter from the fish
1 large onion, peeled and sliced
1 cup of peanut oil for frying (not reflected in nutritional information)

Instructions:

1. Preheat the oil in a large pot or deep fryer.
2. Whisk the eggs and add the onion powder and set aside.
3. In a separate bowl, combine the coconut flour and baking powder and set aside.
4. Dip the fish pieces into the flour mixture, covering both sides, and then into the egg mixture. Place in the peanut oil, and fry for about 5 minutes or more, if needed. Cooking times will depend on the thickness of the fish.
5. While the fish is frying, dip the sliced onions into the egg mixture first this time, and then into the flour. Fry in a separate pot of peanut oil until crispy.
6. Serve the fish and "chips" together with a side of salted malt vinegar.

ETON
MESS (GF, V, H)

HIGH KETO

Difficulty Level: 1 / **Cost:** $
Preparation Time: 20 mins
Cooking Time: None
Serves: 4

NUTRITION FACTS
(Per Serving)

Calories from:

● Fat: 90%
● Protein: 3%
● Carb: 7%

Calories: 440
Total Carbs: 9g
Dietary Fiber: 1g
Protein: 3g
Total Fat: 44g
Net Carbs: 8g

Ingredients:

2 cups strawberries
2 tsp. pure vanilla extract
2 cups heavy whipping cream
1 tsp. liquid stevia

Instructions:

1. Hull the strawberries and add them to a bowl with the vanilla extract and stevia. Stir to coat the berries. Set in the refrigerator.

2. Chill a large mixing bowl inside of the freezer for at least 15 minutes before making the whipped cream. When the bowl is chilled, add the heavy whipping cream, and whip with an electric mixer until peaks form. This can take 15 to 20 minutes.

3. Gently fold in the strawberries and serve.

(Per Serving)

Calories from:
- Fat: 77%
- Protein: 8%
- Carb: 15%

Calories: 106
Total Carbs: 6g
Dietary Fiber: 2g
Protein: 2g
Total Fat: 9g
Net Carbs: 4g

HIGH KETO

MUSHY
PEAS (GF, V, H)

Difficulty Level: 1 / **Cost:** $ **Prep. Time:** 10 minutes
Cooking Time: 5 minutes **Serves:** 4

Ingredients:

1 cup frozen peas

¼ cup heavy cream

1 Tbsp. butter

½ tsp. salt

½ tsp. ground black pepper

Instructions:

1. Add the frozen peas to a pot of boiling water, boil for 5 minutes and drain.

2. Transfer the peas to a food processor with the remaining ingredients and blend until smooth, being careful not to completely puree the peas.

Scottish
CALEDONIAN
CREAM DESSERT (V, H)

Difficulty Level: 1 / **Cost:** $ **Prep. Time:** 10 minutes
Cooking Time: None **Serves:** 4

NUTRITION FACTS

(Per Serving)

Calories from:
- Fat: 92%
- Protein: 4%
- Carb: 4%

Calories: 218
Total Carbs: 2g
Dietary Fiber: 0g
Protein: 2g
Total Fat: 21g
Net Carbs: 2g

HIGH KETO

Ingredients:

½ cup whipped cream cheese

½ cup heavy cream

1 ounce brandy

1 tsp. lemon juice

1 tsp. liquid vanilla crème stevia

Instructions:

1. Place all ingredients in a food processor and blend until smooth and creamy.

2. Serve chilled.

Scottish CAULIFLOWER AND BACON SOUP (H)

HIGH KETO

Difficulty Level: 1 / **Cost:** $$
Preparation Time: 10 mins
Cooking Time: 20 mins
Serves: 5

NUTRITION FACTS
(Per Serving)

Calories from:

- Fat: 77%
- Protein: 12%
- Carb: 11%

Calories: 330
Total Carbs: 12g
Dietary Fiber: 3g
Protein: 10g
Total Fat: 28g
Net Carbs: 9g

SERVING SUGGESTION: Serve with grated parmesan cheese if desired.

Ingredients:

2½ cup vegetable broth

1¼ cup heavy cream

1 onion, peeled and chopped

1 cup chopped bacon

1 head of cauliflower, chopped into florets

Salt and ground pepper to taste

Paprika, for serving

Instructions:

1. Place all ingredients except for the heavy cream into a large stockpot over medium heat and bring to a boil. Simmer for 15 to 20 minutes or until the cauliflower is tender.

2. Using an immersion blender, puree the soup until smooth. Add the heavy cream and stir. Season with salt and black pepper and garnish with paprika.

UNITED KINGDOM

GLAMORGAN
SAUSAGE (GF, H)

HIGH KETO

NUTRITION FACTS
(Per Serving)

Calories from:
● Fat: 75%
● Protein: 15%
● Carb: 10%

Calories: 183
Total Carbs: 7g
Dietary Fiber: 2g
Protein: 7g
Total Fat: 16g
Net Carbs: 5g

SERVING SUGGESTION: Serve with olive oil and a little balsamic, if desired.

Difficulty Level: 1 / **Cost:** $$
Preparation Time: 15 minutes
Cooking Time: 10 minutes
Serves: 8

Ingredients:

Sausage:
½ cup almond flour
½ cup shredded cheese of choice
1 egg
¼ tsp. dried mustard
½ cup shredded leek, sautéed
1 Tbsp. chopped fresh parsley

Coating:
½ cup almond flour
1 egg
4 Tbsp. almond milk
1 Tbsp. coconut oil, for cooking

Instructions:

1. Place all of the sausage ingredients in a large mixing bowl and mix until combined. Roll into 8 small sausages and set aside.
2. Mix the egg and almond milk in a bowl and dip the sausages into the mixture to coat. In a separate bowl, add the almond flour and cover the sausages with the flour.
3. Heat the coconut oil in a large skillet over medium heat and fry the sausages until they are browned on both sides.

Welsh BARA BRITH BREAD (GF, H)

HIGH KETO

Difficulty Level: 2 / **Cost:** $$
Preparation Time: 15 mins
Cooking Time: 90 mins
Serves: 8

NUTRITION FACTS
(Per Serving)

Calories from:

○ Fat: 83%   Calories: 345
○ Protein: 13%   Total Carbs: 9g
● Carb: 5%   Dietary Fiber: 5g
                 Protein: 11g
                 Total Fat: 32g
                 Net Carbs: 4g

READER RECOMMENDATION (PAUL):
Sometimes the simple things in life are the best, just add warm butter. Serve warm with butter.

Ingredients:

2 cups almond flour

1 cup chopped walnuts

1 tsp. allspice

1 tsp. stevia extract

1-inch piece of ginger, grated

1 egg

3 Tbsp. orange zest

1 cup cold brewed tea

1 Tbsp. ground cinnamon

Instructions:

1. Grease a loaf pan with butter or coconut oil, and preheat your oven to 325F.

2. Mix all ingredients together in a mixing bowl and transfer into the loaf pan.

3. Bake for 1½ hours.

Welsh MUSSELS

(GF, M)

MODERATE KETO

Difficulty Level: 2 / **Cost:** $$$
Preparation Time: 15 mins
Cooking Time: 90 mins
Serves: 2

NUTRITION FACTS
(Per Serving)

Calories from:

Fat: 42%   Calories: 298
Protein: 27%   Total Carbs: 16g
Carb: 31%   Dietary Fiber: 1g
                  Protein: 13g
                  Total Fat: 9g
                  Net Carbs: 15g

Ingredients:

20 mussels

1 shallot, peeled and chopped

1 leek, chopped

Lemon juice

Chopped parsley, for garnish

1 cup white wine

1 cup water

½ cup cream

Instructions:

1. Heat the wine and water in a stockpot and cook the leek and shallot.

2. Add the mussels and steam for about 5 minutes. Add the lemon juice, parsley, and cream.

3. Scoop the mussels with the sauce into individual serving bowls, and top with additional parsley, if desired.

NUTRITION FACTS
(Per Serving)

Calories from:
- Fat: 77%
- Protein: 21%
- Carb: 2%

HIGH KETO

Calories: 155
Total Carbs: 1g
Dietary Fiber: 0g
Protein: 11g
Total Fat: 18g
Net Carbs: 1g

Polish-Style
FRIED EGG
BREAKFAST (GF, V, H)

Difficulty Level: 1 / **Cost:** $$ **Prep. Time:** 10 minutes
Cooking Time: 20 minutes **Serves:** 4

Ingredients:

8 eggs
1 cup chanterelle mushrooms
1 Tbsp. butter, for cooking
1 small handful of fresh cilantro
1 tsp. coriander
Salt and ground black pepper, to taste

Instructions:

1. Wash the mushrooms and removing the stems if desired.

2. Add the mushrooms to a frying pan over medium heat with the butter. Fry for about 15 minutes.

3. Add the eggs and continue to fry until the eggs are cooked. Add coriander, salt and black pepper to taste.

4. Serve with fresh cilantro, if desired.

Polish-Style
COFFEE ICE
CREAM DRINK (GF, V, H)

Difficulty Level: 1 / **Cost:** $ **Prep. Time:** 10 minutes
Cooking Time: 5minutes **Serves:** 2

NUTRITION FACTS
(Per Serving)

Calories from:
- Fat: 93%
- Protein: 4%
- Carb: 3%

HIGH KETO

Calories: 310
Total Carbs: 12g
Dietary Fiber: 10g
Protein: 3g
Total Fat: 30g
Net Carbs: 2g

Ingredients:

2 cups dark brewed coffee, chilled
½ cup sugar-free So Delicious coconut-based ice cream
½ cup unsweetened whipped cream (optional)

Instructions:

1. Pour the coffee into the base of 2 large glass cups. Top with 2 small scoops of sugar-free ice cream per cup. Top with whipped cream, if desired.

Polish
DILL PICKLE
SOUP (GF, V, H)

HIGH KETO

Difficulty Level: 1 / **Cost:** $$
Preparation Time: 10 minutes
Cooking Time: 15 minutes
Serves: 8

NUTRITION FACTS
(Per Serving)

Calories from:
- Fat: 85%
- Protein: 6%
- Carb: 8%

Calories: 191
Total Carbs: 5g
Dietary Fiber: 1g
Protein: 3g
Total Fat: 18g
Net Carbs: 4g

Ingredients:

6 cups chicken stock

4 cups dill pickles, chopped

½ cup pickle juice

2 Tbsp. coconut flour

1 cup heavy cream

1 egg

2 Tbsp. clarified butter

8 Tbsp. sour cream, for garnish

Fresh cilantro, minced, for garnish

1 pinch of salt

Instructions:

1. Bring the 6 cups of chicken stock to a boil, and add the pickles and pickle juice. Simmer for 5 minutes.

2. Next, add the coconut flour and heavy cream, and whisk until there are no more clumps of coconut flour.

3. Stir in the egg and butter and simmer for another 10 minutes.

4. Season with salt, and top each serving with cilantro and 1 tablespoon of sour cream.

UKRAINE

Ukrainian
PEA SOUP (GF, V, H)

HIGH KETO

NUTRITION FACTS
(Per Serving)

Calories from:
- Fat: 64%
- Protein: 13%
- Carb: 23%

Calories: 226
Total Carbs: 17g
Dietary Fiber: 5g
Protein: 7g
Total Fat: 15g
Net Carbs: 12g

Difficulty Level: 1 / **Cost:** $$
Preparation Time: 10 minutes
Cooking Time: 90 minutes
Serves: 3

Ingredients:

1½ cups split peas, dried and soaked overnight
1 onion, peeled and chopped
1 Tbsp. tomato paste
½ cup heavy cream
2 cups vegetable broth
1 tsp. salt

Instructions:

1. Place all ingredients in a stockpot, except for the heavy cream, and simmer for 1.5 hours, stirring every half hour.

2. With an immersion blender, blend until smooth. Stir in the heavy cream.

COOKING SUGGESTION:
To soak the split peas, add them to a stockpot and cover with water. Soak them overnight.

Icelandic
COCOA
SOUP (GF, V, H)

Difficulty Level: 1 / **Cost:** $$
Prep. Time: 5 minutes
Cooking Time: 5 minutes
Serves: 4

NUTRITION
(Per Serving)

Calories: 434
Total Carbs: 14g
Dietary Fiber: 5g
Protein: 5g
Total Fat: 43g
Net Carbs: 9g

Ingredients:

2 Tbsp. raw cocoa powder

½ tsp. ground cinnamon

2 tsp. pure vanilla extract

2 cups water

3 cups coconut milk

1 drop liquid vanilla stevia

1 Tbsp. gluten-free cornstarch

Instructions:

1. Pour the water and coconut milk into a saucepan, add the cinnamon and cocoa powder, and whisk.

2. Add the vanilla extract, cornstarch, and stevia.

3. Stir over low heat until warmed throughout, being careful not to burn the milk.

ICELAND

Icelandic-Style
PANCAKES
(GF, V, H)

HIGH KETO

Difficulty Level: 1 / **Cost:** $$
Preparation Time: 10 mins
Cooking Time: 10 mins
Serves: 8

NUTRITION FACTS
(Per Serving)

Calories from:

Fat: 80%   Calories: 417
Protein: 14%   Total Carbs: 13g
Carb: 6%   Dietary Fiber: 7g
                  Protein: 15g
                  Total Fat: 37g
                  Net Carbs: 6g

Ingredients:

3 cups almond flour

3 eggs

3 cups almond milk (unsweetened)

1 tsp. baking powder

1½ tsp. ground cardamom

1 drop liquid vanilla stevia

1 Tbsp. coconut oil, for cooking

Instructions:

1. Add all of the ingredients in a large mixing bowl and whisk until combined.

2. Heat a large skillet over medium heat with the coconut oil, and pour ¼ cup of batter onto the skillet, cooking until the pancake begins to bubble. Flip and cook for an additional 30 to 60 seconds. Continue this process for all of the pancakes.

SERVING SUGGESTION: Roll up the pancakes and fill them with sugar-free strawberry jam for a traditional Icelandic pancake, or top with almonds.

These are best if made into smaller pancakes, but the amount of pancakes per serving will depend on how large or small you make your pancakes. Simply split the total amount by 8.

ICELAND

Icelandic
LOBSTER
BISQUE (GF, H)

HIGH KETO

NUTRITION FACTS
(Per Serving)

Calories from:
- Fat: 68%
- Protein: 27%
- Carb: 6%

Calories: 486
Total Carbs: 8g
Dietary Fiber: 1g
Protein: 32g
Total Fat: 36g
Net Carbs: 7g

Difficulty Level: 2 / **Cost:** $$$
Preparation Time: 20 minutes
Cooking Time: 95 minutes
Serves: 6

Ingredients:

2 pounds shell-on lobster

½ cup butter

2 Tbsp. olive oil

2 carrots, peeled and chopped

1 onion, peeled and chopped

1 Tbsp. tomato paste

1 tsp. cayenne pepper

6 cups vegetable broth

1 cup heavy cream

2 garlic cloves, peeled and minced

1 Tbsp. curry powder

Salt and ground black pepper, to taste

Instructions:

1. Remove the heads and shells from the lobster and chop gently. Heat a large stockpot over medium heat, add the lobster, butter, carrots, garlic, and onion, and sauté for 5 minutes.

2. Add the tomato paste, olive oil, and seasonings and stir. Pour in the vegetable broth and simmer on low for 1½ hours.

3. Add the heavy cream, salt, and black pepper. Use an immersion blender blend until smooth.

Middle East

The recipes featured in this region are traditionally inspired recipes from Israel, Turkey, Lebanon, and Jordan. While the cuisine found in this region is diverse, there are flavors that stay fairly consistent throughout each country.

Beans, parsley, nuts, and seeds are popular additions to recipes in this region. You can expect to see keto-approved ingredients, such as hazelnuts, sesame seeds, and parsley used in many of these recipes. You will also see traditionally keto-inspired recipes made with lots of flavorful spices and nut flours in place of wheat products to keep the traditional flavors in mind. This region contains a healthy balance of light recipes, heavier dishes and, of course, traditionally inspired desserts.

LEMON AND DILL FALAFEL (H)

HIGH KETO

Difficulty Level: 2 / **Cost:** $$
Preparation Time: 20 mins
Cooking Time: 15 mins
Serves: 4

NUTRITION FACTS

(Per Serving)

Calories from:

- Fat: 73%
- Protein: 17%
- Carb: 10%

Calories: 328
Total Carbs: 15g
Dietary Fiber: 7g
Protein: 14g
Total Fat: 26g
Net Carbs: 8g

Ingredients:

1 cup turkey sausage

2 Tbsp. olive oil

½ onion, peeled

2 garlic cloves, peeled and chopped

1 tsp. cumin

¼ tsp. turmeric

½ cup almond flour

Salt and ground black pepper,

to taste

1 cup full-fat, plain Greek yogurt

1 handful fresh dill

1 Tbsp. lemon juice

1 head romaine lettuce, for serving

Instructions:

1. Preheat the oven to 400F and pulse the turkey sausage, onion, garlic, cumin, turmeric and flour together in a food processor. Chill in the refrigerator for 30 minutes.

2. After the mixture has chilled, form 1-inch balls with the mixture, and put aside. Heat a large skillet over medium heat with the olive oil, and cook the falafel balls until brown on both sides, about 1 minute each side. Transfer to a parchment-lined baking sheet, and bake for another 10 minutes.

3. While the falafel is cooking, whisk the Greek yogurt, lemon juice, and dill together. Chop the romaine lettuce for the salad, and divide it among 4 serving plates.

4. Serve the falafel on top of the lettuce and drizzle with the Greek yogurt dressing.

Turkish
TAVUK GOGSU
(CHICKEN BREAST PUDDING)
(GF, H)

HIGH KETO

Difficulty Level: 1 / **Cost:** $$
Preparation Time: 30 minutes
Cooking Time: 20 minutes
Serves: 6

NUTRITION FACTS
(Per Serving)

Calories from:
- Fat: 85%
- Protein: 6%
- Carb: 9%

Calories: 508
Total Carbs: 14g
Dietary Fiber: 3g
Protein: 8g
Total Fat: 49g
Net Carbs: 11g

Ingredients:

1 boneless, skinless chicken breast, cooked and shredded
3½ cups coconut milk
1 cup heavy cream
1 tsp. stevia extract
1 Tbsp. vanilla extract
4 Tbsp. gluten-free cornstarch
Ground cinnamon, for topping

Instructions:

1. Add all of the ingredients, except for the shredded chicken, to a large stockpot over low heat. Simmer until a pudding consistency forms. Add the chicken and stir.

2. Allow the pudding to cool in the pan before serving. Serve in individual bowls with a dash of cinnamon.

SERVING SUGGESTION:
Serve with a dollop of whipped cream as this dish resembles rice pudding serve as a dessert.

NUTRITION FACTS
(Per Serving)

Calories from:
- Fat: 64%
- Protein: 7%
- Carb: 29%

Calories: 53
Total Carbs: 5g
Dietary Fiber: 1g
Protein: 1g
Total Fat: 4g
Net Carbs: 4g

Turkish
SALAD (GF, V, H)

Difficulty Level: 1 / **Cost:** $ **Prep. Time:** 10 minutes
Cooking Time: None **Serves:** 4

HIGH KETO

Ingredients:

1 cup diced tomatoes

1 red bell pepper, diced

1 diced cucumber

1 handful of fresh parsley, chopped

¼ cup lemon juice

1 Tbsp. olive oil

Pinch salt and ground black pepper

Fresh dill, for garnish

Instructions:

1. Place all of the chopped veggies and parsley into a large mixing bowl, and toss with the lemon juice and olive oil.

2. Season with salt and black pepper, and add dill for garnish.

NUTRITION FACTS
(Per Serving)

Calories from:
- Fat: 61%
- Protein: 12%
- Carb: 27%

Calories: 106
Total Carbs: 9g
Dietary Fiber: 2g
Protein: 3g
Total Fat: 7g
Net Carbs: 7g

HIGH KETO

Garlic Yemen
FAVA BEAN
DIP (GF, V, H)

Difficulty Level: 1 / **Cost:** $ **Prep. Time:** 10 minutes
Cooking Time: None **Serves:** 4

Ingredients:

1 cup canned fava beans

3 cloves garlic, peeled and minced

2 Tbsp. clarified butter

¼ tsp. cayenne pepper

2 Tbsp. water

Instructions:

1. Rinse and drain the fava beans and add into a stockpot. Mash with a fork.

2. Add the remaining ingredients and heat over medium heat for 5 to 10 minutes, being very careful not to let it burn.

SERVING SUGGESTION: Serve with fried eggs, vegetables or on an avocado.

Israel-Style
BEET
DIP (V, H)

HIGH KETO

Difficulty Level: 1 / **Cost:** $$
Prep. Time: 5 minutes
Cooking Time: None
Serves: 5

NUTRITION
(Per Serving)

Calories from:
- Fat: 64%
- Protein: 13%
- Carb: 23%

Calories: 167
Total Carbs: 12g
Dietary Fiber: 3g
Protein: 5g
Total Fat: 11g
Net Carbs: 9g

Ingredients:

6 beets, trimmed, peeled and cooked
2 garlic cloves, peeled and chopped
1 cup full-fat plain Greek yogurt
2 Tbsp. olive oil
¼ cup roasted hazelnuts, chopped
¼ cup goat cheese
Cilantro for garnish, if desired

Instructions:

1. Place all of the ingredients in a food processor and blend until smooth.

2. Serve as a spread or with veggies.

JORDAN

MENSAF Jordan LAMB STEW (GF, H)

HIGH KETO

Difficulty Level: 2 / **Cost:** $$$
Preparation Time: 20 minutes
Cooking Time: 40 minutes
Serves: 8

NUTRITION FACTS
(Per Serving)

Calories from:
● Fat: 77%
● Protein: 22%
● Carb: 1%

Calories: 531
Total Carbs: 1g
Dietary Fiber: 0g
Protein: 29g
Total Fat: 45g
Net Carbs: 1g

Ingredients:

4 Tbsp. coconut oil

2 pounds boneless lamb, cut into cubes

4 cups beef cubes

¼ cup pine nuts

1 cup heavy cream

1 tsp. cumin

1 tsp. ground black pepper

¼ tsp. sea salt

Instructions:

1. Place 2 tablespoons of coconut oil in a large skillet, and cook the chopped lamb until cooked through and browned on both sides. Set aside.

2. In a separate skillet, add the 2 remaining tablespoons of coconut oil, and fry the pine nuts for 2 to 3 minutes until brown. Add the beef cubes, heavy cream, and seasonings and stir.

3. Add the lamb to the liquid mixture and simmer for 30 minutes.

Lebanese BABA GHANOUSH (GF, V, M)

MODERATE KETO

Difficulty Level: 1 / **Cost:** $
Preparation Time: 10 mins
Cooking Time: None
Serves: 6

NUTRITION FACTS
(Per Serving)

Calories from:

- Fat: 39%
- Protein: 17%
- Carb: 43%

Calories: 47
Total Carbs: 8g
Dietary Fiber: 3g
Protein: 2g
Total Fat: 2g
Net Carbs: 5g

Ingredients:

1 eggplant, roasted and roughly chopped

8 garlic, peeled

1 Tbsp. lemon juice

1 tsp. stevia extract

2 Tbsp. sesame seeds

1 tsp. coriander

1 tsp. sea salt

Fresh cilantro for garnish

Instructions:

1. Add all of the ingredients to a food processor and process until smooth.

2. Taste and, if needed, add more lemon juice and an additional pinch of salt.

3. Garnish with fresh cilantro

SERVING SUGGESTION:
Serve with your favorite keto-style bread.

Oceania

The recipes for this region focus on Australian cuisine. Australian cuisine has culinary tastes strongly influenced by British, as well as Irish traditions, and wheat has been a staple in the Australian diet since 1788. I have turned traditional Australian recipes into keto-friendly delicious meals while keeping the traditional barbecue recipes in mind to create an authentic Australian flavor.

Australia is also known for growing some of the most popular avocados, which made creating some deliciously creamy ketogenic recipes easy. You will find these recipes to be the perfect balance between sweet and savory while being able to experience what traditional Australian cuisine is all about.

Aussie COLESLAW (V, H)

HIGH KETO

Difficulty Level: 1 / **Cost:** $
Preparation Time: 10 minutes
Cooking Time: None
Serves: 4

NUTRITION FACTS
(Per Serving)

Calories from:
- Fat: 83%
- Protein: 5%
- Carb: 12%

Calories: 267
Total Carbs: 12g
Dietary Fiber: 4g
Protein: 3g
Total Fat: 24g
Net Carbs: 8g

Ingredients:

½ cabbage, green leaves removed, and shredded
1 onion, peeled and chopped
1 carrot, peeled and shredded
½ cup avocado-based mayonnaise
¼ cup full-fat coconut milk
2 Tbsp. red wine vinegar
Juice of 1 lemon

Instructions:

1. Place the cabbage, onion, and carrot into a mixing bowl.

2. In a separate mixing bowl, whisk together the coconut milk, mayonnaise, red wine vinegar, and the lemon juice.

3. Pour the dressing over the cabbage mixture and stir until combined.

OCEANIA

HIGH KETO

Australian
SHRIMP ON
THE BARBIE (GF, H)

Difficulty Level: 1 / **Cost:** $$
Preparation Time: 20 mins
Cooking Time: 5 mins
Serves: 4

NUTRITION FACTS
(Per Serving)

Calories from:

○ Fat: 92%   Calories: 289
○ Protein: 7%   Total Carbs: 1g
● Carb: 1%   Dietary Fiber: 0g
                          Protein: 5g
                          Total Fat: 30g
                          Net Carbs: 1g

Ingredients:

20 king prawns or jumbo shrimp
2 Tbsp. olive oil
½ cup butter, melted
¼ cup fresh parsley, chopped
2 Tbsp. lemon juice
2 garlic cloves, peeled and chopped
Mint leaves and fresh limes, for
garnish

Instructions:

1. Combine all of the ingredients, except for the shrimp and mint leaves, in a mixing bowl, and stir.

2. Add the shrimp to the sauce, and let this sit for 15 minutes.

3. Preheat your barbecue and place the shrimp on skewers. Grill for about 2 minutes on each side.

4. Garnish with fresh mint and lime, if desired.

Australian

CREAM OF
MACADAMIA SOUP (GF, V, H)

HIGH KETO

Difficulty Level: 1 / **Cost:** $$
Preparation Time: 10 minutes
Cooking Time: 60 minutes
Serves: 4

NUTRITION FACTS
(Per Serving)

Calories from:
- Fat: 88%
- Protein: 5%
- Carb: 7%

Calories: 423
Total Carbs: 11g
Dietary Fiber: 3g
Protein: 5g
Total Fat: 43g
Net Carbs: 8g

Ingredients:

4 carrots, peeled chopped

1 leek (white portion only)

2 garlic cloves, peeled

1 cup macadamia nuts, finely chopped or ground

4 Tbsp. butter

4 cups chicken broth

¼ cup heavy cream

2 Tbsp. chopped fresh cilantro (reserving 1 Tbsp. for garnish)

1 tsp. turmeric

1 tsp. salt

½ tsp. ground black pepper

Instructions:

1. Add all of the ingredients, starting with the butter, to a large stockpot. Bring to a boil, and then reduce heat and simmer for 1 hour.

2. Using an immersion blender, blend until the soup is very smooth.

3. Garnish with fresh cilantro, if desired.

READER RECOMMENDATION (JOAN):
This creamy soup works well as the base for many different soup variations by swapping out the turmeric and adding any spices of your choice.

Australian
AVOCADO
SMOOTHIE (GF, V, H)

HIGH KETO

Difficulty Level: 1 / **Cost:** $$
Preparation Time: 5 minutes
Cooking Time: None
Serves: 1

NUTRITION FACTS
(Per Serving)

Calories from:
- Fat: 87%
- Protein: 5%
- Carb: 8%

Calories: 409
Total Carbs: 17g
Dietary Fiber: 9g
Protein: 5g
Total Fat: 39g
Net Carbs: 8g

Ingredients:

½ cup full-fat coconut milk

½ cup coconut water

½ avocado

¼ cup baby spinach

1 handful of fresh parsley

1 drop stevia extract

Instructions:

1. Place all of the ingredients in a blender and blend until smooth.

Keto-Style ANZAC BISCUITS (GF, V, H)

HIGH KETO

Difficulty Level: 1 / **Cost:** $$
Prep. Time: 10 minutes
Cooking Time: 20 minutes
Serves: 12

NUTRITION
(Per Serving)

Calories from:
- Fat: 87%
- Protein: 10%
- Carb: 3%

Calories: 244
Total Carbs: 5g
Dietary Fiber: 3g
Protein: 6g
Total Fat: 24g
Net Carbs: 2g

Ingredients:

2 cups almond flour
¾ cup shredded coconut
1 tsp. baking soda
1 tsp. stevia
½ cup (1 stick) butter

Instructions:

1. Preheat your oven to 350°F.
2. Mix the almond flour and shredded coconut together.
3. In a large saucepan over low heat, mix the butter, baking soda, and stevia until the butter has melted.
4. Add the butter mixture to the dry ingredients, and stir.
5. Drop 1 teaspoon-sized cookies onto a parchment lined baking sheet, and cook for 18 minutes or until golden brown.

Printed in Great Britain
by Amazon